The Agile Manager's Guide To

RETAINING EMPLOYEES

The Agile Manager's Guide To

RETAINING EMPLOYEES

By Ken Tanner

Velocity Business Publishing
Bristol, Vermont USA

For Jennifer, Renae, and Katherine, the other women in my life

Copyright © 2001 by Ken Tanner
All Rights Reserved
Library of Congress Catalog Card Number: 2001092506
ISBN 1-58099-032-0
Title page illustration by Elayne Sears

Printed in Canada

If you'd like additional copies of this book or a catalog of books in the Agile Manager Series®, please get in touch.

- **Write us:**
  Velocity Business Publishing, Inc.
  15 Main Street
  Bristol, VT 05443 USA

- **Call us:**
  1-888-805-8600 in North America (toll-free)
  1-802-453-6669 from all other countries

- **Fax us:**
  1-802-453-2164

- **E-mail us:**
  action@agilemanager.com

- **Visit our Web site:**
  www.agilemanager.com

Ken Tanner operates an Atlanta-based consulting firm specializing in recruiting, team building, and retention. He is also available for seminars and speaking engagements. Ken invites your contact at klt@consultant.com.

Contents

Introduction 7

1. Why Focus on Retention 11

2. Recognize Discontent 19

3. Start Them Off Right 35

4. What Employees Need 51

5. Provide the Basics 61

6. Relationships with Managers and
   Co-Workers 79

7. Enable Personal Fulfillment 93

8. Fight Back 111

Coda 125

Books in the Agile Manager Series®:

Giving Great Presentations
Understanding Financial Statements
Motivating People
Making Effective Decisions
Leadership
Goal-Setting and Achievement
Delegating Work
Cutting Costs
Influencing People
Effective Performance Appraisals
Writing to Get Action
Recruiting Excellence
Building and Leading Teams
Getting Organized
Extraordinary Customer Service
Customer-Focused Selling
Managing Irritating People
Coaching to Maximize Performance
Managing Change
Retaining Employees

Introduction

Treat people as adults. Treat them as partners; treat them with dignity; treat them with respect. Treat them—not capital spending and automation—as the primary source of productivity gains.

—TOM PETERS AND ROBERT H. WATERMAN,
IN SEARCH OF EXCELLENCE

My baptism into the critical nature of retaining employees came when I was contracted by a company to redesign its recruiting program. Try as it might, it just couldn't keep positions filled. It wanted my advice for creating innovative methods for attracting quality employees.

My first step was to examine past practices. I asked to see the files for everyone hired in the past three years. An hour later, over two hundred files were carted into my work area. And this was a company of seventy-five people!

I immediately delivered my analysis. "There is no recruiting problem here," I announced. "You're *great* at recruiting. You just can't keep the people you hire." We changed the scope of that project, focusing on plugging the hole in the bucket rather than continually refilling it.

I have seen many companies describe their staffing problems as an issue with attracting people, when the obvious issue is retention. In fact, the only time most managers think about retention is when they receive a resignation from an employee. **Yet you must realize that attrition will attack, damage, and even kill the most successful companies. You cannot achieve your long-term goals if turnover is commonplace within your organization. Period.**

But we have some battles to fight to hold on to our people. The current economy makes some people confident that they can easily find something else if their job doesn't work out. Many companies have replaced traditional pension plans with portable 401(k) retirement plans, reducing some of the financial risk of frequent job changes. The Internet makes it easy for people to find out about other jobs, even while sitting in the office of their current employer. And the executive search industry has grown recently, so employees are more likely than before to have someone approach them with attractive new jobs.

A worker may occupy a cubicle at Lockheed, Microsoft, or McCleskey's Auto Parts, but where is his heart? Today, workers offer their loyalty to their professions rather than to their companies. In these days of free agency, a player measures his worth as a point guard or a quarterback, not as a Laker or a Philly.

But the fact is, people *do* want to pledge allegiance to something. The desire to belong is a basic value. It allows corporate logos to be prominently displayed on personal clothing, motivates gang membership, and even persuades soldiers to storm a beach. Employees do prefer to stay with their companies. The companies just need to learn how to quit running them off.

Most companies show little attention to the loss of their talent. For instance, if a $2,000 computer disappears from an employee's desk, I guarantee there will be an investigation and all heck will break loose. But what happens when a $100,000 executive with critical client relationships gets stolen by a competitor? No one investigates the cause. No one is called on the carpet for it. No one is trained to prevent it from happening again. Why, we usually throw the executive an incredible going-away party!

Still other companies, in a retention effort that runs a mile wide and an inch deep, think it's effective to adopt all the fad-of-the-week programs managers read about in yesterday's edition of *USA Today*. They pull lots of motivational programs right off the shelf, allowing employees to bring their parrot to work, empowering their people by entrusting them with music selection for the company holiday party, instituting Friday afternoon beer busts, and calling everyone a *partner*. But when it comes to taking serious steps to deal with managers who run roughshod over people, or getting rid of ridiculous policies and procedures, or ensuring that a quality benefit package is provided, executive heads dive into the sand.

Indeed, while 75 percent of senior executives say that employee retention is a major concern, only 15 percent have made it a strategic priority. That degree of management nonfeasance dismays me. What if an oil company stated that its depletion of oil reserves was a "major concern" yet failed to make it a strategic priority? Imagine the stockholder revolt!

How bad will things have to get before companies wake up? The average public company loses half its workforce every two years. By 2010, the population of workers aged thirty-five to forty-four is expected to decrease by 15 percent. There will be 161 million jobs but only 154 million people in the workforce. Even if a company can absorb the tremendous costs associated with losing an employee, there soon won't be anybody left to hire.

You cannot stop attrition by just pulling some methods off the shelf and inserting miscellaneous programs. You must have an overall corporate culture consistent with the principles discussed in this book. And it must be a sincere commitment.

This book, then, is for those serious about retaining the team they have developed. You could be an owner of a small business, the head of a department of a major company, or an entry-level manager trying to hold onto the team you just inherited. True, some of the advice talks about lofty corporate-wide programs, benefits, and policies that you may have no control over. But the spirit of the book—the focus on respecting your employees and providing for their individual needs—is a universal solution.

Besides, if you adopt the spirit of the book and do a great job in retaining your team members, there is a good chance you eventually *will* have control over determining your company's lofty corporate-wide programs, benefits, and policies. Mastery of this subject will make just such an impact on your employees' lives, your company's future, and on your career.

Chapter One

Why Focus on Retention?

"Federal Express, from its inception, has put its people first both because it is the right thing to do and because it is good business as well."

—FRED SMITH

"So, what you are telling me is that this is a temporary assignment. I'll be coming right back to this position as soon as I straighten out their problems. Right?" The Agile Manager wanted absolute assurance from his boss that this project was actually a reward, not a way to move him out the door because of the recent merger.

"Absolutely!" replied Jim. "Look, when we merged with this company, we had no idea how terrible their turnover problem was. I mean, everybody has staffing problems these days, but this company is running nearly twice the industry rate."

"That is a problem," the Agile Manager agreed. "But why me? I'm not in human resources. I'm a manager." As soon as he said those words, the Agile Manager realized it was not one of his smarter statements. He corrected himself: "Well, I guess management is 90 percent human resources, isn't it?"

"That's right," replied Jim. "Here are the facts. You have built one *of the most solid teams our company has ever known. Turnover has been virtually nonexistent over the last six years. I don't think that was by accident."*

The Agile Manager smiled and thought to himself. You'd better believe it wasn't by accident. Just recently he had had to put in special effort when the merger came down. In fact, he had almost even lost his trusted second in command, Wanda.

"Teambuilding is just one benefit of retention," he told Jim. "There are a lot more. In fact, if we were to just add up the dollars that turnover costs this company . . ."

Not long ago there was great excitement at the Martin & Newby Electric Shop in London. A twenty-five-watt light bulb, hanging by a naked wire from the ceiling of the entrance way, burned out. The bulb had been burning for seventy-one years.

That light bulb was a rarity; most bulbs of today last only a year or two, if that. There are employees like that light bulb, staying at one place for their entire careers. But these people have become about as rare as the British bulb. Today, average job tenure is 3½ years and dropping fast.

So, why should we be concerned? Light bulbs can be replaced, and so can people.

This attitude worked well up until 1990, but we all acknowledge that that statement is ludicrous today. You know that employees are hard to find. But have you ever considered all the problems that worker attrition causes? Let's first look at the dollars involved.

When all factors are considered, replacement costs for an average staff or clerical position averages about 150 percent of the departing person's annual salary. An extreme example: One company with a large national sales force estimates that it costs about $1 million whenever a salesperson leaves. And this does not include the departed employee's attempts to take the company's customers over to his new company.

Does this seem *too* extreme? Let's look at some of these costs and how they can add up to such a significant amount.

The Direct Costs of Replacement

There are some turnover costs that are immediately evident and easy to identify. Consider the cost of recruitment. This includes the cost of advertisement, time for processing and even the big money that people like me charge you to find key executives. These are some simple statements, but recruitment costs alone can equal half of an executive's annual salary.

That is, of course, if the new employee is hired in at the same salary as the one being replaced. This is usually not the case. The new executive will probably be given a higher salary than his predecessor. Many other expenses, such as social security taxes, will also increase since they are indexed to the salary. Plus, many new workers require a signing bonus and other cost-of-entry benefits.

The biggest direct cost will probably be relocation. It is not unusual to pay $100,000 for all expenses to relocate a mid-level executive, especially if a home equity buyout is required.

Best Tip

Remember: The cost of replacing an employee averages 150 percent of the position's annual salary.

Training costs continue to add to the tally. The training programs, cost of trainers and the worker's salary during this non-productive time add significantly to the cost.

The Indirect Costs of Turnover

Since some costs of turnover are "indirect," they are easily ignored. That's a big mistake. Indirect or not, they still represent cash. For instance, what is the financial impact on your company for the decreased productivity from someone who is looking for a job? His lowered work ethic? The impact this person has on the morale of his co-workers? Late assignments? Non-contributions at meetings?

Soon-to-leave-employees often miss work for interviews and also tend to come in late and leave early. They are also likely to use company time to surf the Internet looking for job opportunities.

What's more, you need "fill in" help during the gap between the employee's termination date and the hiring date of a new one, which could mean hiring temps or increasing overtime costs.

Now consider the silent costs associated with replacing the terminating employee. How much productivity is lost in the workplace while his replacement is trained and brought up to speed? Look at all the productivity lost just by hiring the new worker, including the time used by secretaries, interviewers, human resource executives and co-workers. (How many clerical, staff, and administrative positions could be saved if your turnover were cut in half?)

Best Tip

Don't overlook indirect costs when figuring the cost of turnover. They can be as significant as the direct costs.

And then there is the impact on morale when someone leaves for greener pastures and the possibility that the terminated employee will take people with him. You should also realize that when an employee leaves for another position, headhunters smell blood in the water. Just like sharks, they make a beeline for your company, sensing an atmosphere that may encourage additional employee defection.

The Impact on Customers

Customer satisfaction is dramatically affected when talented, productive employees leave. Marriott Corporation has found a direct relationship between employee and customer turnover. It found that decreasing employee turnover by 10 percent decreases customer turnover 1 to 3 percent. A comparable Small Business Administration study found that decreasing employee turnover 15 percent had a 25 percent impact on pre-tax profits. New hires will make mistakes that can lose customers. And customers often use this learning curve as an opportunity to explore other suppliers.

And that is just the result of losing customers through *dissatisfaction.* Calculate the effect on your business when a salesman actively recruits your customers to join him at his new employer. And what are the cumulative effects of his simply saying bad things about your company?

The Loss of Intellectual Capital

We don't need to focus on just the obvious costs in losing salespeople. Other employees might be even costlier. The real wealth of many a company rests in its collection of intellectual capital, the special knowledge of its people. Consider a research scientist at a pharmaceutical company, a chemist with a perfume company, or even the head chef at a popular restaurant. Calculating the exact costs of losing these people may be impossible, but they do unquestionably represent a serious portion of the company's net worth.

And that's just for "routine" terminations. What about key executives? One *Fortune* 50 company estimates the cost of losing a product-development team leader at $29 million! This is due to the necessity of getting a product rapidly to market and the lost opportunity for income as the project stalls while the company finds a new leader. But even this is peanuts when you think of the industry giants. What would happen to the value of Microsoft stock if Bill Gates were to leave?

Best Tip

Don't wait for a "retention crisis" to force you to create a retention program. Do it now before the damage is done.

Many companies wait until they have a retention crisis before focusing on turnover. This is a shortsighted management practice. **You do not have to have a turnover problem to reap the benefits of lowered turnover.** Read the case of SAS on the next page. Its turnover was one-fourth that of the rest of the industry. Yet when it considers the enormous losses caused by just one

---

RETENTION IN ACTION

Direct costs can add up. And cutting your turnover rate can increase your bottom line dramatically. For instance, SAS Institute, the world's largest privately held software company, has more than 6,700 employees.

Even though it has locations around the globe, it has achieved a turnover rate of less than 5 percent, compared with an industry rate of 20 percent. This magnificent retention rate saves SAS about $50 million in hiring and training costs annually. That $50,000,000 goes straight to the bottom line.

And employee loyalty pays dividends, literally. At the stock brokerage firm A. G. Edwards, the broker retention rate is 92 percent compared to the industry average of 80 percent. Edwards also has a higher *customer* retention rate than the industry average, and it is the most profitable firm in the brokerage industry.

---

turnover, SAS continues to focus heavily on the issue. Reducing turnover even a few percentage points will have an enormous impact on your company's profitability.

The Impact on Profits

Up to now, this chapter has focused on the dollar cost of turnover. But there is a more significant reason to improve retention. Here is a fact: The best companies, those who consistently return money to their shareholders, have low turnover. I am not certain which is the cause and which is the effect, but there is an absolute, undeniable correlation.

For example, compare the companies featured in two annual lists: *Fortune* magazine's *Most Admired Companies* and Levering and Moskowitz's list of *The 100 Best Companies to Work for in*

America. Then observe their profitability. There is an amazing over-lap. The same names seem to appear on all the lists. Remember this fact: High retention equals high profits. Every time.

Now that you understand the high cost of turnover, let's focus on what you can do to keep people satisfied and productive for the long term.

The Agile Manager's Checklist

✔ Turnover costs you a lot more money than you think. Commit now to reducing it.

✔ Turnover has direct costs, like the cost of hiring a recruiter or advertising. It also has many indirect costs, like missed work and lowered morale.

✔ In today's world of knowledge work, each departing employee carries with him or her valuable intellectual capital.

✔ Never forget: The better the retention rate, the better the profits.

Chapter Two

Recognize Discontent

"You can buy a person's time; you can buy their physical presence at a given place; you can even buy a measured number of their skilled muscular motions per hour. But you can not buy enthusiasm. You cannot buy loyalty. You cannot buy the devotion of hearts, minds, or souls. You must earn these."

—CLARENCE FRANCIS

The Agile Manager was on his way to pick up his rental car. He did not particularly enjoy eavesdropping, but there was no way to avoid overhearing a delicious conversation between two women on the airport shuttle. "So what's the story with Larry Wood?"

"He just waltzed in last Tuesday, packed up his office and said 'hasta la vista, baby!'"

"That must have been a surprise."

"It's never a surprise when someone leaves anymore. Scott Johnson is an absolute jerk. He's practically cleared out the whole department in the last year."

"Why do you stay?"

"They're paying me more than I could get anywhere else. That's *the only way they can get anyone to work for the guy." She laughed like Glenn Close as Cruella De Vil. "But I'll only put up with it until I can find something else."*

"I know what you mean," the other woman replied. "There aren't many happy campers in my department, either. Everyone is grumbling about something. If it's not their boss, it's the benefits or the boring work or the lack of recognition. I'll bet the place is a ghost town in six months!" The women rose to get their luggage and exit the van. "And you know what's so ridiculous? The company doesn't have a clue how upset we all are."

Wow, the Agile Manager thought. And I thought I had problems! He was taking some relief in the misery of others when he noticed the tag on one of the women's luggage pieces. It featured his company's logo.

Despondent over his unsuccessful boycott of companies supporting Taft-Hartley legislation, my Uncle Alfred decided to run off and join a monastery. This religious order took a vow of silence. In fact, they were only allowed to speak two words every ten years. In 1957, Uncle Alfred was summoned before the head monk and allowed to speak his two words. "Bed hard," he stated.

Ten years later he was again given his two spoken words. "Food cold," he declared. The head monk nodded and he was sent back to his work. Ten more years passed and on May 27, 1977, he made his statement: "I quit."

"I'm not a bit surprised," the head monk declared. "You've been complaining ever since you got here."

The head monk was a rarity: a manager who actually saw a resignation coming. Most managers are surprised when handed a resignation. But if managers are to become better at reducing turnover, they must have the skill to recognize discontent within the workforce.

Managers should not be shocked when an employee quits. Rarely does someone change jobs without first displaying some early warning signs. Poor managers overlook inconsistent behavior, or write it off to "a phase they are going through." A good manager knows her people and can immediately sense when they are behaving in a different manner.

Watch for inconsistent behavior in these areas:

Attitude. Perhaps the first indication is in attitude. Someone with a reputation as a cheerleader begins complaining about even the slightest problems. She develops a "who cares?" attitude or becomes apathetic when others complain. You may see her suddenly shift her focus from finding solutions to dwelling on problems.

Productivity. Note any rapid drop in productivity. Someone who regularly works long hours becomes a clock watcher. The person who was always eager to take on new challenges no longer volunteers for projects. Observe behavior at meetings. A regular contributor during meetings now rarely speaks, and she stops championing her positions.

Absences. Also, it is hard for people interviewing for another job to hide this fact. Just look for the signs. They start dressing better. They request vacation one day at a time. A person who is rarely absent begins using sick days, especially on Fridays or Mondays. Likewise, she frequently takes time off on afternoons.

Best Tip

If you're shocked when an employee quits, you haven't been paying attention. Watch especially for changes in attitude.

Dilbert. And here is the latest indicator of job dissatisfaction: The employee starts to post an enormous number of *Dilbert* cartoons in his cubicle or office. These people are not simply displaying their great sense of humor. They are trying to send a message. Pay heed and sit them down for a chat.

Watch for Life Changes

Things happen to us that often prompt reexamination of our lives. Often, the first thing that people look at changing is their jobs. Watch for the events listed below. If one occurs, it is a good time to sit down with the employee and take her temperature:

- A mentor, boss, or friend leaves the company.
- There is a major re-organization.
- Her last child graduates from high school or college.
- She receives an advanced degree.
- She turns forty (or thirty or fifty).
- There is a divorce or death in the family.
- She is rejected for job promotion.
- She sells all of her company stock.

Listen to Your Employees

What is the best way to determine who might be looking for another job? Ask people to tell you. As you are routinely chatting with your employees (i.e., *Management By Wandering Around*), casually ask if they know of anyone who seems dissatisfied or who may be looking for another job. In fact, ask if they are themselves happy with the company. You will be surprised how many people will respond honestly to this direct inquiry. Indeed, they may have been looking for an opportunity to talk about it. Make it easy for them to discuss the subject.

Best Tip

When chatting with employees casually, ask, "Do you know of anyone who's dissatisfied or looking for a job?"

You should ask newly hired employees why they decided to come to work at your company. Make a note of the reason and follow up regularly to see if those expectations are being met. This will help you catch discontent at its earliest stage.

You can also ask your business partners. For instance, consultants are often approached and asked about how to become a consultant. Vendors are sometimes asked if they know of jobs available elsewhere. Ask your consultants and other outside vendors if anyone has approached them about such possibilities.

Have regular brainstorming sessions with your management team. Discuss who you think may be vulnerable and why. One indicator may lead nowhere, but the input of several people may paint an obvious picture. Force-rank your employees as to how the group perceives vulnerability of each. Then take action.

You can also become proactive and actually search for people who may be looking actively for a job. Here are some ways to do this. (You should decide for yourself which methods are, in your own mind, ethical. But before you get all wadded up over this, remember that your goal is to save an employee and the end may indeed justify the means. Your call.)

- Identify the office gossip and ask him to tell you when he thinks someone is looking.
- Search the Web's job boards for the resumés of your employees.
- Check to see if the resumé on the person's personal Web site has been updated recently.
- Have a headhunter call the person directly and see how interested he is in talking.
- Look at previous job changes to see if there is a predictable pattern.
- Run a blind ad in the newspaper. Any of your employees who answer must be quite dissatisfied—and desperate. (Please use this information to save the employee, not for the development of a loyalty list.)
- Have your HR department notify you when employees ask "quitting-related" questions. (How does COBRA work? How are 401(k) funds transferred?) Do not let your HR department refuse this reasonable request by claiming that the inquiry is "confidential."

Avoid Gripe Sessions

I hate gripe sessions. Hate, hate, hate, hate, hate them. You know the scenario. Once a year, someone from HR will come in at the end of the meeting and announce that management wants to know what you *really* think. They may even ask any higher-ups to leave the room, so that the remaining peers will feel free to talk openly. Then he'll turn to a flip chart and announce, "OK, who wants to start us off? Anyone? Anyone?"

Soon, people feel guilty that they can't think of anything that's upsetting them. So they think of something. Anything to break the awkward silence. Meanwhile, the one employee suffering from morale retardation sees his chance and begins leading the assault with some obscure issue. ("Why is the toilet paper such a cheap grade? Don't they care about us enough to spend an extra dollar on toilet paper? And what about the color they painted the lunchroom? We all hate beige.") The others nervously nod their agreement, because they are team players and want to look like they're participating. Eventually, you wind up with a list of gripes that no one realized was upsetting them, and a lot of employees that did not know, until that moment, that they were unhappy.

Gripe sessions are amateur psychological exercises. And, just as with all layman attempts at playing psychologist, the results do more harm than good. Remember a basic premise of management communication—good news and training in groups, bad news and reprimands in private. Gripe sessions, by their definition, are negative and demoralizing. If you want to know what your people think (and I am sure that you do), use some of the other methods described in this section. Or better yet, ask them. One on one.

Ask 'The Question'

Those of you who have read *The Agile Manager's Guide to Recruiting Excellence* know that I have one question I ask everyone I try to recruit. The Question is: *If you were to leave and go work for another company, what would probably be the reason?*

This question flushes out a person's prime motivation. You can identify her needs. When you use it with your current employees, it will also help you identify your vulnerabilities. Try using this question as you chat with your employees. It will give you a good understanding of their mindsets.

RETENTION IN ACTION: UPS

It is no accident that a typical UPS television commercial features one of its drivers. This is because the delivery driver is the key to UPS's relationship with its customers. He gets to know the clients personally, their needs, and their patterns of service. This virtually assures that UPS will be the carrier of choice when their clients are deciding whom to ship a package with.

UPS wisely determined that it was important to their marketing efforts that they reduce driver attrition as much as possible. They used exit interviews and confidential surveys to learn the main reasons drivers quit. Was it money? Long hours? Mean bosses? No. The biggest reason for driver loss was they didn't like the exhausting task of loading the trucks at the beginning of their shift.

UPS responded by changing the job. They hired a whole new crew of employees just to load the trucks. The drivers now begin each day fresh. They are able to concentrate on their relationship with the customer instead of dreading the daily grind of lifting boxes. And, they add about an hour a day doing what they are most effective at: delivering packages and interacting with the customers.

The turnover in the loading job is now 400 percent a year, but it's far easier to fill those positions than it is to find reliable drivers. While UPS didn't increase overall retention, it did reduce turnover where it had the greatest impact on the organization.

Conduct Nontraditional Exit Interviews

Many companies use exit interviews to determine the actual reasons employees quit. Unfortunately, the traditional exit interview is as useless as the third verse in a Baptist hymnal. Routine questionnaires handed to employees on their last day do a poor job of uncovering the real reasons someone leaves. This is because they fail to differentiate between the factors that make the new job attractive to the employee versus the reasons that made the employee vulnerable to leaving in the first place. These are usually two different things!

For instance, most employees list "more money" as their primary reason for leaving. But if you dig deeper, you will discover that an employee was not unhappy with her salary when a headhunter approached her. She was actually dissatisfied with some other aspect of her job, often the relationship with her boss. However, she does not report this as the reason on the exit interview, fearing that she will be labeled a troublemaker, or maybe because she just doesn't want the potential conflict. So instead of reporting what was *wrong* with her old job, she states what is *right* with her new job. (This is why, by the way, that so many counteroffers fail. The company addresses the wrong problem.)

As we will discuss later, the real reason for an employee leaving is most often dissatisfaction with her boss. And who is it that usually has the employee fill out the exit interview? Yep, the boss.

Exit interviews can serve a valuable purpose to the organization. Charting them can lead to important trends to be addressed and situations that must be corrected. But they are worthless if they do not produce accurate information. Even worse, they can be costly if they point you in the wrong direction.

Here are two important things to remember in using exit interviews. First, conduct them two to three months after the employee has left. This will remove the "threat" from the exercise and the answers will be more candid.

Second, use a third party to conduct and collect the interviews. Although using the mail has some security (as opposed to filling out the form under someone's watchful eye), it is best if the ex-employee is sending the form to someone outside of the company. Again, the ex-employee is more apt to be honest with her answers. Perhaps more importantly, those answers will be interpreted and analyzed by an impartial person. Let's get real. If a manager is getting bad reports on her personally, what are the chances that she'll accurately report the problem?

Exit interviews can occasionally serve another positive purpose, if they are sent out a few months after the termination. Between sixty and ninety days out, many new employees begin to realize that the grass really isn't greener in other pastures. This is a time of second thoughts and regrets. The person is quite vulnerable to a suggestion that she return to her old job. Your contact at this time may motivate the ex-employee to inquire about coming back to your company.

On the next page you'll find a sample exit interview document.

Do Regular Culture Surveys

The exit interview is a good way to find out why people leave, but it is somewhat like vaccinating a corpse. A culture survey, on the other hand, is helpful in taking the temperature of your current workforce and uncovering danger signals of unhealthy situations.

I have included a sample of a culture survey on pages 30, 31, and 32. However, realize that an effective survey features questions that are customized to fit a particular company. Your survey should likewise be targeted to the issues most affecting your organization.

Best Tip

Conduct exit interviews a few months after the person's departure. They'll be more forthcoming with information.

Use an outside firm to conduct this survey. This will allow confidential communication and impartial tabulation. If you cannot use an outside firm, at least use an external mailing address to

Exit Interview

Will you do us one final favor? We were sorry to see you leave. We have built our industry-leading reputation because of excellent people like you. Will you help us by telling us about your decision to leave?

Please answer these questions and place the form in the envelope provided. It will be delivered to Ken Tanner & Associates, an independent consulting firm, for tabulation. **Your responses will remain confidential.**

What was the primary reason for your decision to leave our company?

Were you actively seeking another job, directly approached by your new company, or called by a recruiter?

How would you describe the morale of your work group?

How would you describe your manager or supervisor?

How would you rate the salary and benefits at your new job compared to our company?

What could we have done to keep you with our company?

Is there anything else that we should know about your decision to leave?

NOTE: Perhaps your new job is not quite what you expected. Please call Jennifer at 678 555-1996 if you would like to discuss returning to our company. There's no obligation, of course, and our chat will be held in total confidence.

collect the surveys. You will not receive credible feedback if the employee believes she'll be handing the form back to her boss.

So, how do you interpret the data? Is an overall score of 87 percent good? I don't know. The fact is, you can't draw a trend line until you have at least two points. You'll need to do the survey regularly in order to determine your trends. Only then will you know if your action planning is successful. I recommend that the survey be done each year. And be sure to ask the same questions each time so that the data can be analyzed properly and compared accurately.

While you need more than one survey to compare your progress as a whole, you can compare the questions to each other to determine your strengths and weaknesses. You don't need a Ph.D. to interpret your results if the average score is 88 percent, *good health benefits* scores a 95 percent but *My manager is friendly and easy to talk with* comes in at 45 percent.

Again, hire an outside firm to tabulate and analyze the data. You will be surprised at how revealing and useful the information will be if an experienced, independent consultant oversees the process.

Don't keep the results of the survey an upper-management secret. You must share all the information, results, and conclusions with your employees. They will want to know the results as much as you do.

Realize that the administration of a culture survey will set up certain expectations. Employees will be disillusioned—perhaps angry—if you perform this survey and then don't do anything with the information. Take action. No, that does not mean that you give the employees everything they ask for. But it does mean that you seriously consider their input and tell them the reasons if you will not make some of the changes they expected.

If you respond to employees needs, react to their concerns, and listen to their thoughts, the culture survey will be a tremendous morale booster and retention tool. If you fail at this, however, it will become a useless exercise at best and an *attrition* tool at worst.

Statement	1	2	3	4	5	6
I have fun working here.	☐	☐	☐	☐	☐	☐
I feel good about the teamwork in my department.	☐	☐	☐	☐	☐	☐
There are open and honest communications within my department.	☐	☐	☐	☐	☐	☐
ABC values me.	☐	☐	☐	☐	☐	☐
I receive the recognition that I deserve.	☐	☐	☐	☐	☐	☐
Company policies are fair and they are consistently enforced.	☐	☐	☐	☐	☐	☐
I would recommend ABC as a place of employment to my friends.	☐	☐	☐	☐	☐	☐
I am proud to work for this Company.	☐	☐	☐	☐	☐	☐
I am treated with dignity and respect in all situations.	☐	☐	☐	☐	☐	☐
This company is committed to the highest standards of ethics.	☐	☐	☐	☐	☐	☐
ABC offers me good career advancement opportunities.	☐	☐	☐	☐	☐	☐

Please go on to the next page to complete the survey.

ABC Company Culture Survey

Please rate the following statements based on two things. How important is this item to you?
And to what degree do you agree or disagree with the statement?

Importance
1=Important
2=Neutral
3=Not Important

Agree or Disagree
1=Strongly Agree
2=Agree
3=Somewhat Agree
4=Somewhat Disagree
5=Disagree
6=Strongly Disagree

	Importance			Statement	Agree or Disagree					
	1	2	3		1	2	3	4	5	6
	☐	☐	☐	I am given the training I need to do my job well.	☐	☐	☐	☐	☐	☐
	☐	☐	☐	My manager gives me the feedback I need to do my job.	☐	☐	☐	☐	☐	☐
	☐	☐	☐	My manager is friendly and easy to talk with.	☐	☐	☐	☐	☐	☐
	☐	☐	☐	My manager listens to my ideas.	☐	☐	☐	☐	☐	☐
	☐	☐	☐	I am paid fairly for the work I perform.	☐	☐	☐	☐	☐	☐
	☐	☐	☐	My pay is competitive with what other companies pay.	☐	☐	☐	☐	☐	☐
	☐	☐	☐	ABC Company offers good health benefits.	☐	☐	☐	☐	☐	☐
	☐	☐	☐	My last performance evaluation was fair and accurate.	☐	☐	☐	☐	☐	☐
	☐	☐	☐	This company cares about me.	☐	☐	☐	☐	☐	☐

ABC Company Culture Survey

Department: _____

Here is what I like best about my job:

Here is what I like the least about my job:

If I were to be made president of this company, here is the first thing I would change:

If I were to leave this company and take a job somewhere else, this would probably be the reason:

Thanks for your participation!

Now What?

OK, using the techniques listed here, you've ferreted out discontent. Now what do you do? If an employee has just told you he or she has taken another job, skip ahead to chapter eight—Fight Back. If the situation is not dire, then read on at a leisurely pace. Retaining employees, you'll see, is a process and not a single act or event. Once you understand what people need from a job, you can tailor individual responses to specific management retention challenges—or head them off altogether by creating programs designed to satisfy employees before they get itchy feet.

The Agile Manager's Checklist

✔ Employees send out warning signals when they are discontented. Make it a point to look for reduced commitment and productivity.
✔ Engage in frequent casual conversations with your people. You'll uncover problems in the making.
✔ Conduct culture surveys on a regular basis. It's akin to taking the company's temperature.
✔ Act on what you find out through surveys and conversations.

Chapter Three

Start Them Off Right

"Hire fast, suffer slow."

—ANONYMOUS

It was day three on the job and the Agile Manager was wrapping up his initial analysis of the branch's attrition problems. A review of the files showed one telling statistic. Over 80 percent of the employees who quit did so within the first ninety days.

The Agile Manager had lunch with an employee he had met several years earlier at a legal seminar. He outlined his findings to her.

"That's not really surprising," Annelise stated. "In fact, I still can't believe I lasted past the first week."

"Tell me how were you introduced to the company," the Agile Manager prompted.

She put down her fork, leaned back and chuckled. "I smile about it now, but I refer to it as the Orientation from Hell. The first thing that happened was that some nineteen-year-old intern from human resources sat me down with the Employees' Welcome Manual—which was really just a list of rules and ways that the company *could fire me—and I had fifteen minutes to read and sign it. I then saw an orientation video . . . lots of music and logos, no information. Then the intern had me spend several hours filling out forms and releases. A quick lunch—alone—and then I was taken to my cubicle, which had no office supplies, phone lists, or passwords. I was given a stack of manuals and reports to read until my boss could get with me. Unfortunately he was out of town until Thursday. I felt like I was in Paris and I couldn't speak French."*

"Wow. It is a wonder that you stayed, said the Agile Manager. "Has anything changed since you went through it?"

"As a matter of fact, something significant did change," Annelise replied. "The intern quit."

I was doing an initial consultation with an HR director. He showed me a chart which graphed the turnover of hourly employees during their first ninety days. Over the previous four years, this turnover rate had increased in a straight line from 5 percent to over 20 percent. He commented that he has been trying to use this statistic to convince top management that entry-level wages had to be increased.

There were two problems with his analysis. First, his company already paid some of the best wages in its industry. (In fact, it was fourth out of thirty major companies.) And second, these people were quitting in the first ninety days, for Pete's sake. They knew the wage when they accepted the job and none could have expected a pay increase that soon.

No, this company's problem was desperation hiring. Because critical positions were empty, the company was filling them quickly. And, in order to bring on people as quickly as possible, they lowered their hiring standards. Then, these lower-standard people created issues, causing more people to quit. The company, again wanting to quickly address the problem, hired in more new people, usually with even lower standards. This cycle continued to its present state. Turnover begets turnover.

Retention Begins with the Hiring

One of the problems we have with selection is that we evaluate candidates on their ability to *get* the job rather than on how they will *do* the job. Our selection process often evaluates the person's handshake, presentation, and poise as opposed to looking at job skills and cultural fit. Then we are surprised when this splendid candidate becomes an incompetent employee.

A tremendous amount of turnover occurs within the first ninety days of employment. Now, three months is just not enough time for someone to get into any real trouble, so the problem with early terminations generally rests with the recruiting and selection process. I recommend that you read *The Agile Manager's Guide to Recruiting Excellence*[1] to learn an effective recruiting method that leads to better retention. But let me review some key principles for those of you who have not yet read the book or are too thrifty to buy a copy.

Turnover often happens within the first ninety days. Therefore, set clear standards and be patient to avoid hiring duds.

Know who you are looking for. You must write a realistic and thorough job description, including the personal and cultural traits you need. You will not get a good fit if you fail to do this. If you do not have a good fit, the person will leave your company.

Cast a wide net. Use multiple sources to attract quality candidates. This will assure a greater likelihood that you will see more people who meet your needs.

Evaluate people on job-related criteria. Use your job description to evaluate your candidates. Too many people evaluate candidates based on non-job related criteria, such as their sense of humor, the way they dress, or just how darn confident they seem to be. Develop your criteria before you begin interviewing and let these point you to the right hiring decision.

---

[1]Yes, this is the first, of many, shameless plugs.

Verify, verify, verify. Some candidates say things that are not true. Some candidates are good at pulling the wool over people's eyes. Some candidates are not what they seem to be. Sound obvious? Probably so, but I'll bet everyone in a management position has gotten burned at least once by failing to verify a candidate's claims. Check references and credentials.

Ask tenure-related questions. Part of your interview with the candidate should be dedicated to assuring yourself that he is apt to stay with your company. As you ask about each job on his resumé, ask the candidate why he decided to go to work for the company. Ask about his decision to leave each job. Also, probe into the candidate's response to conflict. Like all animals, people under stress will either fight or flee. A history of fleeing may indicate that he'll jump ship whenever the going gets tough.

Smooth the Transition

Many new employees are lost in the period between acceptance of the offer and the targeted start date. This is often due to the mishandling of a critical time—the transition period. This time is filled with counteroffers, teenagers livid about moving to a new town, and second thoughts about the wisdom of the decision. Moving to a new job is a tough process. Make it easy for the new employee to make the transition into your company. Let's discuss some ways to do this.

Go ahead and get any paperwork filled out before the actual start date. This paperwork includes all the government forms, but more importantly should include forms for insurance and benefit packages. Why not wait? Because many employees are lost before they actually start work thanks to counteroffers from current employers. Processing administrative papers mentally commits the employee and moves him past the second thoughts many experience during the transition.

Get the spouse involved at this time and communicate directly with her. This will serve multiple purposes. First, the spouse should have the benefit package explained in person and any questions answered directly. The fact is that the new employee often fails to pass along information that the spouse finds important. But this involvement also helps solidify the hire by bringing the spouse into the company's family.

If relocation is involved, have someone contact the spouse and offer assistance. Take full advantage of the excellent relocation services offered by professional moving companies. Furnish extensive information about the new city, school districts, and real estate prices. Consider getting the spouses and kids of your current employees to help orient the family to the community.

Pay a lot of attention to the family's needs during the first three months of employment. Do not let the family feel it is isolated and on its own during this time. It is a time of tremendous stress and you should accept responsibility for relieving it.

Best Tip

To avoid hiring job hoppers, find out in interviews why a candidate left one job for another.

Get as much information to new hires as soon as possible. Here are some ways you can do that before employees actually start. Notice that these ideas will help recruits feel they are a part of your company and feel comfortable even before they are on the payroll.

- Issue the company car, laptop computer, etc.
- Give them their e-mail address, password, telephone number, ID card, corporate credit card, etc.
- Allow them access to corporate web pages so they can begin the learning curve before they actually start the job.
- Assign them a departmental "mentor" to assist them during the first month in getting answers they need.
- Give them a telephone directory updated with their name in it.
- Ask them who they would like to meet during their first week. Schedule the meetings before they start.

- Have their business cards delivered to their house before their first day.
- Assign a mentor and have that person contact the new employee before the start date. The mentor can prearrange meeting with new peers, provide a full facility tour, etc. This will establish a personal bond even before the new hire is on the payroll.

Prepare Your Organization

How you introduce new employees to the company—and their new subordinates—is a critical step in assuring their success with your company. Your new hire could be a shock for some people if you conducted the search confidentially. Also, you must manage the feelings of any internal candidates that were passed over. This is of special importance if these internal candidates will be reporting to your new employee. Do all within your power to assure the new employee is given a positive introduction.

Provide an Excellent Introduction

Think of every cliché you have heard about the importance of a first impression. Then multiply by a factor of a hundred. That will come close to describing the importance of the orientation.

To avoid losing an employee before she even starts, have her fill out the paperwork. It'll create a sense of commitment.

A poor orientation turns into a disaster if it contradicts the initial impression woven through the hiring process. Almost all companies do an orientation for new employees but few pay much attention to them. New employees come to work excited about the prospect of a new job only to get cold water splashed in their faces the first day.

A negative first impression takes months to overcome. Research shows that improving orientation can increase retention rates by as much as 25 percent. Initial frustration also slows time to productivity, increases error rates, and can take the enthusiasm out of any new hire. Let's look at an orientation process that serves to promote goodwill instead of terrifying the new employee.

Use This Orientation Outline

There is not, of course, any boilerplate orientation program. But let me propose a program as described below. Note what it is not. It is not a session to sign papers and issue keys. (This should really be done before the person actually starts work.) Rather, the orientation is an opportunity to explain how things are done, how to be productive, and what the

Best Tip

Introduce the new employee to the veterans properly— especially if some of them were passed over for the job.

company is all about. Does this sound like a lot of meaningless theory? Look at my proposed outline on the next page and see just how practical it really is.

You should, of course, use this only as a starting point to develop your own orientation program. My point is not to promote specific meeting agenda items. It is to show you how to separate the bookkeeping and technical aspects of bringing someone on board (i.e., filling out the stinking paperwork) from the indoctrination. Don't miss this opportunity to give the new employee a solid introduction to your company.

Who Should Conduct the Orientation?

Many companies have the orientation conducted by the human resources department. Don't do this. Have the orientation conducted by the manager and peers within the new employee's department. It is said that a bird will bond with whomever it first sees upon hatching. It's a stretch, but new employees are often the same way. Who do you want him to bond with, his manager and peers or an HR intern?

Managers and employees should own the orientation process

Orientation Outline

THE COMPANY'S CULTURE

- Who's who: the organization chart
- Company culture: history, mission statement, future vision
- How to align personal and organizational strategy and goals
- The cultural no-no's
- The leadership practices most valued by senior management
- What keeps company execs up at night?
- How the company rewards and recognizes individual and team contributions

THE COMPANY'S BUSINESS

- Industry and market trends and challenges
- Strategic direction and medium-range plans
- How the company makes a profit
- Company divisions and channels and how they connect

DAY-TO-DAY OPERATIONS

- Basic business protocol
- Requesting help and support in an appropriate manner
- Appropriate e-mail and voicemail etiquette
- Meeting involvement and contributions
- Executive protocol

MANAGING YOUR CAREER

- Taking charge of growth and professional development

- Identifying personal strengths and skills
- Identifying personal developmental opportunities
- Making the best use of your time
- Performance feedback and evaluation
- Communicating and marketing your successes
- Coaching and mentoring others

and take responsibility for getting new team members up to acceptable productivity because they are closer to the problem and will suffer the consequences if it is not done correctly.

Explain Your Expectations

You should meet with your new employee no later than the first day of work and explain your expectations for him. Outline your goals, review the job description, and explain the standards of performance. Set high standards from the start. If you have a set format for performance reviews, show him the format and discuss the areas that will be reviewed.

Let your new employee know, from the beginning, detailed performance expectations and why he is critical to the organization. Discuss even the simplest things; you would be surprised how much people assume when left to their own resources to figure out how things work in a new company.

Involve the Family

I have mentioned this concept several times, but let me expound a bit on involving the family. People consult their families before changing jobs, and it is to your advantage that they be supportive of your company. This can be especially useful if you are hiring entry-level workers or teenagers. If you are hiring a lot of teenagers, such as for a fast-food company, make it a habit to telephone or meet with the parents when you hire them. Tell the parents that you take your responsibility as an employer seriously, and that you will teach their child good work habits and

Retention in Action: Southwest Airlines

Southwest is the only airline I actually *enjoy* flying. That is because of the cheery, polite people who work for it. Ticket agents, flight attendants, even the telephone reservationists star as goodwill ambassadors for the airline. How do they attract such people?

Besides the fact that outstanding candidates tend to flock to companies that have outstanding employees, Southwest has an interviewing system that allows it to really get to know its applicants. This system features a behavior-based, conversational style of interviewing that puts people at ease. Applicants feel like they are talking to a friend and they are open and honest with their responses.

For example, one applicant was asked how he dealt with conflict with his co-workers. He was so relaxed that he admitted to stabbing one with a screwdriver. But more than a screening tool for psychos, Southwest's interview process brings out indicators of how successfully a candidate will fit into the airline's customer-focused culture.

After intense analysis of the behavior of its own employees, Southwest has developed questions to test for the specific needs and requirements of each job, as well as for shared attributes such as common sense and good judgement.

The system works. Southwest will hire 5,000 people in a typical year. This group is culled from 160,000 applicants and 70,000 interviews. Does its process work? Southwest has the lowest turnover in the airline industry—less than 9 percent. Few would argue that it is this stability that makes Southwest's service the highest rated among the major carriers.

skills. Let them know that they should feel free to call you at any time if they ever have any questions or concerns. In short, win over the parents. I assure you that when the worker is feeling stressed and considers quitting, the parent will intercede and often save this employee.

Train Your New Employee Thoroughly

You will be eager to get your new employee up and running as soon as possible. This eagerness may prompt you to place the employee in a death spiral if you fail to give him the proper training.

Commit to giving your new employee full training, letting him learn all aspects of the new job. I have seen too many people fail in a new job because they were not allowed the opportunity to learn the system before they were held responsible for managing it. Do not make this amateur mistake.

Recognize the Critical Days for Retention

Orientation involves more than the activities surrounding the first day of employment. The vast majority of employees that last for ninety days will likely become long-term employees. So, it makes sense for you to extend orientation-type activities throughout this period. Make note of days that are particularly critical to the retention of the employee during their first three months.

Hiring day. The first critical day is the day the employee is hired. Make a big deal out of the job offer. Stress how important the person will be to the organization and how much you are looking forward to her joining the team. The key here is to let the person put on a cloak of identity; she has become a part of something.

If a uniform is part of the new job, this is the time to provide her with it. Stress what the uniform symbolizes: She is now a part of the team. No one does this better than the Marine Corps, by the way. They go so far as to let the new recruit know that the Marine Corp will never die, so, by putting on the uniform, *he* will never die. I cannot recommend you get *that* dramatic in your presentation, but don't be afraid to wax philosophic to some degree.

First day of work. The next critical day is the first day of work. We have covered this to some degree, but let me add one important element. Perform a debriefing at the end of the day. It does not have to be anything formal, but sit down with her and chat for five or ten minutes. "How did your first day go? How were you treated? Were there any surprises? Do you have any questions or concerns?"

Best Tip

Don't skimp on training new employees. Without good training, the employee's chances of failing are higher.

First impressions make up most of our perception about things, and the first day on the job will have incredible influence on her feelings about it. Have this discussion and catch problems early.

First payday. Their first payday is a big moment in a new employee's tenure. This is especially true if this also happens to be her first job. Personally present the employee's paycheck. Sit down with her and explain the check. Show the hours worked, verify that the pay rate is as you agreed. And then discuss the deductions. Take special time discussing the taxes, including social security. Most people have no real comprehension of how large a bite this is. Also discuss any deduction for benefits.

First month on the job. You should again meet with the employee again after her first month. This is another debriefing, but should be a bit more extensive this time. Employees are pretty much into the swing of things by now; much of the initial training has been completed, and they have met all their co-workers and have assimilated themselves into the team. Lots of impressions have been made by them and about them. It's a great time to talk.

I would even recommend that you do an informal, unofficial performance review. Review the objectives you had for them and discuss how these have been handled. Discuss any problems that have been uncovered. Again, this is an early discussion so they can be discussed without too much discomfort. And then get feedback from the employee.

Three months on the job. We discussed earlier that the ninety-

RETENTION IN ACTION: 'OUTSIDE THE BOX' RECRUITING STRATEGIES

A good way to reduce turnover is to actively recruit people who belong to demographic groups that are not prone to quit. Here are some successful strategies in action:

—Microboard Processing recruits at-risk applicants such as former drug abusers. The company starts these new employees on simpler tasks before moving them inside to the assembly operation. The employee becomes used to the discipline of work, while the company can assess the employee's work ethic. In return, the company gets some hardworking employees who appreciate the opportunity to rebuild their lives.

—Locate your company outside of the common business areas. For instance, high-tech companies often cluster in Silicon Valley. Doing so makes it easy for competitors to steal their employees. However, consider locating your high-tech company in a small town far from California where these particular skills are not in high demand. For employees with young families, the idea of relocating to a smaller community may be quite appealing. They put down roots. And, they rarely quit because competitor companies would require relocation.

—No sector has been hit harder than the restaurant industry in finding enough qualified people. McDonald's and Wendy's pioneered the recruitment of physically and mentally challenged employees to staff many of their positions. Soon, just about every other chain followed, finding that these workers not only performed their work in an exceptional manner, they also demonstrated a superior work ethic. They arrived on time, worked hard, and were loyal. In short, they valued their jobs. This all added up to low turnover rates in an industry legendary for its attrition.

day mark is a milestone. Most people who last ninety days stay to become long-term employees. This is indeed a cause for celebration. Do so. Bring in a cake and a few party favors and have a brief celebration at the beginning of the day. It doesn't have to be a big event. It's the acknowledgment of peers that will mean a lot. If yours is a large company, you may consider a luncheon each month honoring those reaching their ninety-day mark.

Celebrate the Arrival of New Employees

You will evolve your own formal process for welcoming a new employee. Following the procedures I've previously outlined will certainly give a professional and thorough introduction. But why not go beyond the practical and proper? Try some ideas that will add to the experience, make it memorable, and even help shape your company's culture.

Here are some ideas for you to adapt to welcome new employees to your company, area or department:

- Have the CEO contact new employees on their first day. This could be by phone or a drop-by meeting in the CEO's office.
- Sponsor a new-hire luncheon on the first day to meet the team.
- Place a welcome banner on the recruit's cubicle signed by the whole team.
- Take a team picture on the first day.
- Place an advertisement in the local newspaper to let everyone know you have new team members, just like law firms do.
- Send spouses and children first-day welcome gifts.
- Have other spouses call and welcome the spouse of a new hire.
- Give new hires a reserved parking spot to celebrate their first week.

- Give them license plate covers for their cars announcing their new company.
- Send an e-mail (from their computer) to all employees announcing their arrival. List hobbies, interests and other facts about the new employee, encouraging others to reply. This will serve as a great icebreaker and quickly introduce them to many people with which they have much in common.

The Agile Manager's Checklist

✔ Remember that retention begins with hiring. Hire well, and you'll improve retention.

✔ Involve spouses in the transition to a new job. You'll gain a potent ally.

✔ Conduct a thorough orientation. It'll pay for itself many times over.

✔ First day, first week, first month: all are critical days in your attempt to keep employees happy for the long term.

Chapter Four

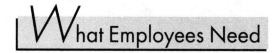

What Employees Need

"To succeed you need to find something to hold on to, something to motivate you, something to inspire you."

—Tony Dorsett

The Agile Manager had only been back from lunch for about an hour when Scott—the "jerk" he'd heard about on the shuttle—came to see him to discuss yet another resignation. It was the lady on the bus with the Cruella De Vil laugh.

"She came to see me this morning and handed me her notice. I couldn't believe it. I didn't even see this one coming." Scott continued, explaining that Alexandra had been a strong worker and even covered for much of the slack when positions were left open. "I've always been able to count on her. This is a real shock."

"Where is she going to work?" the Agile Manager asked.

"MegaGlobal. And you know what? She'll be making the same amount of money as she did here!" Scott seemed genuinely amazed. "So, here is what I'm going to do. I'm going to make her a counteroffer with a 10 percent raise. That ought to keep her with our team."

The Agile Manager winced at Scott's use of the word "team."

"Let's discuss this a bit more before you do that. Since she is not leaving for more money, I doubt offering her a raise will address her reason for quitting." The Agile Manager got up and closed the door to his office. "Now, let's talk about how to keep Alexandra with us, beginning with one critically important issue. The MegaGlobal job is giving her something she wants that we aren't providing. Let's figure out what that is."

A few weeks after he had divorced the opera singer[1], my cousin Ralph took a long walk through the woods and contemplated his life. Suddenly, a frog jumped into his path and sat right in front of him. The frog spoke: "Please sir. I am not really a frog, but a princess. A wicked witch placed this curse upon me. If you will kiss me, I will turn into a beautiful woman and serve you the rest of my life."

"Well, I'll be," my cousin muttered. He reached down, picked up the frog and gently put her into his pocket.

"What are you doing?" asked the frog. "I told you that if you kissed me, I would become a beautiful princess!"

"I realize that," Ralph replied. "But at this point in my life, I think I would rather have a talking frog."

While this chapter does discuss a lot of theory (relax—we'll keep it light and hold it to just a few pages), it does set up the principles needed to understand how you can hold on to your employees. The bottom line is this: **People stay with companies that meet their needs.** Simple enough, but the real trick is knowing what people want.

This is where the well-intentioned manager screws up. She wants to take care of her people and wants to provide for their needs. She practices the Golden Rule, treating them just as she would want to be treated. And they quit faster than she can hire them. What happened?

Unquestionably, the greatest interference to understanding em-

---

[1] See *The Agile Manager's Guide to Recruiting Excellence,* page 100. This is yet another shameless plug.

ployees has been caused by the Golden Rule. Now, before I am burned at the stake as a heretic, let's review what the Golden Rule says. *Do unto others as you would have them do unto you.* Do you see the disjoint here? If you follow the Golden Rule, you will be treating others as *you* want to be treated, not how *they* want to be treated!

For instance, if you are motivated by title and prestige, you may try to take care of your employees by giving them grand titles and locating them in plush offices. But this will do nothing to satisfy someone who is motivated by job security and good medical benefits for her sick child. Ergo, the long-term employee who wants stock options doesn't have the same concerns as the new parent, who would be happier and more productive with more time off or a flexible schedule.

Understand that I am asking you to violate yet another basic management principle. Remember the one that says that in order to be fair you must treat all employees the same? Toss it out the window. People have different needs and they must be handled differently.

What are these needs? There have been a lot of motivational theories over the past fifty years but, surprisingly, they all seem to say the same thing. Let's review some Psychology 101, which does a good job of putting things in perspective.

Maslow's Hierarchy of Needs

In 1943, Abraham Maslow published his model arguing that the behavior of individuals at a particular moment is determined by their strongest unsatisfied need[2]. These needs begin at the most basic and rise to the spiritual.

Physiological Needs. These are our most basic requirements for life, food, clothing, shelter, oxygen, and water.

Safety Needs. Once our physiological needs are satisfied, we become concerned about our own safety. In other words, we will risk our lives to obtain food if we are starving. We will risk death

---

[2] Douglas McGregor also used Maslow's Hierarchy of Needs to construct his popular Theory X and Theory Y.

for a glass of water if we are stranded in a desert. But once these basic needs are obtained, the list of things we'll die for becomes short indeed. We then devote our attention to safety and security.

Social Needs. Once our bellies are full and we feel secure, humans will reach out for relationships. People are naturally social and like to interact and be with others in situations where they feel they belong and are accepted.

| **Best Tip**

The new golden rule at work: Treat people as *they* would like to be treated—not as *you* would like to be treated.

Esteem Needs. The need for esteem (or recognition) appears in a number of forms, including prestige and power. Prestige is the conduct that other people are expected to show in one's presence: the degree of respect or disrespect, formality or informality, reserve or frankness. Power is the resource that enables a person to induce compliance from or influence others. While these behaviors are sometimes seen in animals (such as lion pack dominance or chicken pecking order), this is the level that begins separating humans from the rest of the ark.

Self-Actualization Needs. Now we are examining a strictly human trait. Self-actualization is the need to maximize one's potential, whatever that may be. As Maslow put it "What a man can be, he must be." This need is the most mature one and can only be sought when all other needs have been met. This explains why a lawyer at the top of her profession drops out of her career track and becomes an artist, or why a hospital chief of staff resigns to join the Peace Corps.

Uncle Sam's Hierarchy

According to a 1998 Labor Department survey, these are the top eight things workers want from their jobs.

1. Career opportunities
2. Challenging job
3. Feeling valued

4. Recognition

5. Relationship with their managers

6. Friendship with colleagues

7. Job security

8. Money and benefits

Are we noticing a pattern here? This is almost amazing; the top eight needs voiced by American workers in 1998 match Maslow's Hierarchy of Needs exactly. Management theory actually reflects reality.

Let's Put It All Together

Just so that we have all this (literally) on the same page, let's classify the needs of your employee as well as outline the next three chapters:

MASLOW	UNCLE SAM	THE AGILE MANAGER
Physiological Needs	Money, Benefits	Basics
Safety Needs	Job Security	
Social Needs	Friendships with Colleagues Relationships with Managers	Relationships
Self-Esteem Needs	Recognition Feeling Valued	Personal Fulfillment
Self Actualization Needs	Challenging Job, Career	

Attend to Generational Needs

There is another thing we must look at in understanding our employees' needs—the generation they belong to. Once again, this discussion is an extreme generalization. Some Gen Xers may be focused on retirement while many mature workers may be seeking a new entrepreneurial challenge. But looking at the generations serves as a good starting point.

Let's look at the three generations that currently make up our workforce and explore some of their common needs.

The Greatest Generation

Born before 1945, this generation has had predictable career paths, worked hard for one or two companies, and moved up the ladder playing by the rules. They are loyal, risk-averse and possess a Capraesque[3] work ethic. These older employees have years of experience and are a valuable asset. You should value them for what they know, not just what they do. We'll go into considerable more detail on this generation in chapter eight, but for now make these observations.

> **Best Tip**
>
> Keep Baby Boomers happy by providing security, training, flexibility in how jobholders approach the job, and help in planning for retirement.

- **Work with Social Security to maximize compensation.** Workers under seventy will see their Social Security benefits reduced dramatically if they earn too much additional compensation. Learn the details about this and work with each individual to minimize the impact on total income.
- **Teach them new skills.** It is a mistake to assume that older workers are set in their ways and cannot learn new skills. They enjoy challenges and learning new things. Train them

---

[3] I.E., ethics as seen in the movies of Frank Capra. You know—he's the guy who directed *It's a Wonderful Life.*

as you would any other worker.

- **Understand their need for a higher quality of life.** They have spent a career working long hours. While they want to work less, they don't want to come to a complete stop. Develop part-time opportunities for them so that they can remain active and you can continue to benefit from their experience.

Baby Boomers

The "ME" generation, born between the end of World War II and the Kennedy assassination, represents a majority of middle and upper management. They grew up at a time of economic prosperity and political skepticism. Baby Boomers like to win, be in control, and make an impact. Boomers tend to focus on themselves. You must provide incentives that Boomers will value.

- **Benefits.** There is a strong need for security in this group that often translates thorough medical coverage and other vehicles for protecting the money they have accumulated.
- **Retirement planning.** Many boomers experience anxiety over their financial future. Companies can offer help with retirement planning, pension benefits, and realistic financial planning. They prefer a gradual retirement rather than the traditional retirement upon hitting the age of sixty-five.
- **Leisure.** They demand time for leisure activities and family, and look for part-time, job sharing, flextime, or other flexible opportunities.
- **Training.** Keeping up to speed, especially in the area of technology, is a notable challenge for many boomer workers. Effective training can minimize employee burnout, job obsolescence, and career plateauing.

Boomers began their careers with the rally cry, *He who dies with the most toys wins!* They are ending their career with the argument, *He who dies with the most toys is still dead.* This generation is experiencing a tremendous reversal in their view of life, focusing more on family, leisure, and self-actualization.

Generation X

Generally the children of Baby Boomers, this generation (born between 1964 and 1981) was raised during their parents' turbulent and self-centered years. Ergo, they tend to be fiercely independent, resourceful, and skeptical of authority.

This is a notoriously difficult group to retain. In fact, they are often referred to as hummingbirds because they flutter from job to job. Although they may be committed while working for a company, they will never display blind loyalty. Instead, their loyalty is to their profession. They expect an exciting and challenging environment and also seek a personal life outside of work.

- **Flexible work arrangements.** Xers grew up without much supervision. Employers must offer autonomy, flextime, job sharing, telecommuting, sabbaticals, and so on.
- **Skill development.** Xers eagerly seek to learn new skills, both to keep the job exciting and to increase their marketability. Ongoing training, especially in technological skills, is often a requirement for employment.
- **Feedback.** Generation Xers' love feedback. Although they want to work independently, they also seek time with their managers to show what they have done and get the manager's approval.
- **Solicit their opinions.** This generation likes to feel appreciated and want their opinions valued. They indicate that the number one quality they want in a boss is *someone who listens.* Beg them for their opinions and then demonstrate compassionate listening skills.
- **Show me the money.** You will be most successful with Gen Xers by providing immediate and tangible rewards, such as money, dinner certificates, and tickets to cultural events.

- **Have fun.** This group wants the balance they saw missing from their parents' lives. Incentives and benefits that demonstrate an organization's support of a balance are noticed and given great value in deciding on an employer.

The Agile Manager's Checklist

✔ Never forget: People stay with companies that meet their needs.

✔ Don't treat all employees the same. Cater to their different needs and interests.

✔ Another part of the motivational puzzle is understanding that Baby Boomers, Gen Xers, and those of the Greatest Generation all have different concerns.

Chapter Five

*P*rovide the Basics

"The lack of money is the root of all evil."

—GEORGE BERNARD SHAW

"Yes. I am aware of how Scott—and everyone else over there—uses money to keep people," Wanda stated coldly. "In fact, we are all aware of it."

The Agile Manager could actually hear Wanda frown as she made that statement. He had called her to get a weekly update on his department back home and had been discussing some of the challenges he was facing. Wanda was always someone who could splash cold water on him when he needed it. Today was no exception. "What do you mean?" he asked. "It sounds like the grapevine has been working overtime."

"Of course", she replied. "We all compared salaries when the merger took place. We were shocked at how much more that company paid for the same job compared to us. And then we learned why. Every time someone quit, they were offered a lot more money to stay. Word would get out, and everyone threatened to quit unless their pay got adjusted. You can see how that spiraled."

Indeed he had. The Agile Manager thought through the situa-

tion. He had an unstable workforce, heavy attrition, and uncon-scionable pay rates. These people were making the top money in the industry but they were still unhappy. And now the unfair com-pensation rates threatened to spill over into his company because of the merger. What a mess. "Do you have any advice?" he asked Wanda.

Of course she did. "Yeah. Tell them that they have more than one tool in their shed. Use them."

Basics include salary and benefits, of course, but also include addressing the employee's need for job security. These are core requirements for the worker. If not addressed, expensive reten-tion programs that highlight promotions, pride, and picnics will be a waste of money. Let's look at these basic needs, starting with money.

Compensation

Employee surveys rarely list salary as their number one incen-tive. Because of this, it has become the vogue to completely over-look salary in analyzing employee satisfaction. However, while salary is never the number one priority, it certainly is regularly on the top ten list. And, unlike every other entry on the list, sal-ary is the one factor that no em-ployee would ever work without.

Best Tip

Do what you must to make workers feel secure in their jobs. It's just as impor-tant as salary and other compensation.

While I have pretty much dedicated the rest of this book to telling you that there is much more to retention than just money, we need to strike a bal-ance. I find that it is a pass/fail issue. Compensation must allow a certain standard of living, but beyond that point other factors become more important. (This is in complete agreement with Maslow's theories on motivation.)

Despite this, managers still think of money as the cure-all for solving employee loyalty problems. We see this when making counteroffers to people who are resigning. The company will decide that the way to keep the employee is to give them more money. But money is rarely the primary reason for a person changing jobs. In fact, it only becomes the prime factor when the offer is substantial, usually more than 20 percent[1].

Let's cut to the chase on money. It is not the most important item unless your employee is making less working for you than he could make working for the *majority* of your competitors. Keep your compensation competitive and you will rarely have money-based attrition.

Best Tip

Keep your salaries competitive and your company will rarely have turnover based on issues of compensation.

There is an exception to this. You may choose to base your recruiting efforts on extremely high compensation plans. Though I cannot recommend it, you can attract a strong workforce if you set a structure that is about 20 percent greater than your average competitor. But pay-based incentives carry great peril. The problem with pay-based incentives is that there is always someone willing to pay more. Also, if money is the only tool in your box, you will attract a mercenary workforce that cannot be motivated in any manner other than cash. You must be prepared to stick with this structure no matter what the economic times or the condition of the company. If workers are attracted solely by money, they will jump ship in a heartbeat if the attraction is reduced.

Many books have been written and studies conducted examining both the theory as well as the practical execution of compensation. I am going to disappoint you greatly if you felt that I

---

[1] And let's face facts. If you have been *underpaying* someone by this much, you probably have some even greater problems to deal with and it is to the employee's best interest to get out of your organization. And if your compensation has been fair but someone else is willing to *overpay* by this much, you should probably congratulate the employee for his good fortune and wish him the best.

was going to give you the answers to establishing pay rates in a competitive market. This book just isn't thick enough and I'm not smart enough to do that for you. But let me give you these thoughts on setting salaries and pay rates:

Pay a good wage. In fact, page an excellent wage. You should target to be in the 75th percentile in your industry. If you are at this level, you can usually be assured that any turnover issues are caused by factors other than salary.

Best Tip

To encourage retention, tie bonuses to sticking with the job. Do that by spreading bonus payments for a year over the *following* year.

Keep abreast of what others are paying. Pay scales constantly fluctuate within industries. Today's excellent compensation may not be so two years later. You can keep informed of what competitors are paying by looking at their advertisements, culling information from applicants, and even asking headhunters. (But **do not** directly ask your competitors what they are paying. Our helpful federal government may interpret this as collusion and find you in violation of all sorts of wicked regulations.)

Tie bonuses to tenure. Supplemental compensation plans, such as bonuses, should encourage retention. Base your objectives on annual performance and spread the payments out over the following year. By the time the employee has collected this bonus, he is well into the next bonus period and will have an incentive to stick around for that payment.

If you worry that delayed payments may diminish the impact of bonus rewards, consider a program conducted by **Sega Software** that offers interesting retention impact. Sega offers bonus recipients the *option* to defer all or part of the bonus for one year. If so, they will mark up the deferred reward by 50%. If they defer payment for two years the company will double payout. However, workers forfeit the bonus if they leave the company.

Also, consider using incentives that help underscore tenure. Rather than cash, use stock options that mature in the future. While their award provides instant gratification for the recipient, their true value does not exist until the worker has been retained for the long term.

Offer retroactive pay raises. I find a White Castle Restaurant wage program to be quite clever. They piggyback on the idea that if a worker stays with the company for ninety days, he is likely to become a long-term employee. So, to encourage workers to stay during this vulnerable period, they deliver a *retroactive* pay raise at the ninety-day anniversary. This increase is in the fifty-cent range and pays them a lump sum for all hours worked to that point.

Benefits

I am reminded of a cartoon I saw years ago. An executive is being presented with a job offer and the HR manager said, "Of course with all these benefits, there will be no salary."

Benefits have grown to be a large percentage of a worker's compensation package. It's not unusual to find the value of benefits exceeding 50 percent of the worker's salary.

While there was a time in which benefits were considered extras and referred to as "perks," they are now an expected part of the package. Let's touch on some of the more popular benefits[2].

Medical insurance. This is an absolute requirement if you have any intention of keeping a quality workforce.

Vacation. Another requirement if you want your position to be considered a "real" job. Standard vacation policies are generally two weeks after one year of service, three weeks after five, and four weeks after ten.

---

[2] This is not meant to be an exhaustive analysis of different benefits. Rather, I am making a few comments about some of the benefits that may be offered and strongly suggest you seek advice from appropriate professionals when structuring your specific benefit package.

Holidays. This has also become a standard benefit, but holidays celebrated vary greatly. Thanksgiving and Christmas are absolutes, but as many as nine other holidays are sometimes added by larger companies. One current vogue—giving employees their birthdays off.

Sometimes holidays are mixed with personal days, allowing the employee to decide what specific days to take off. (For instance, Jewish workers may prefer days off during their religious holidays rather than around Easter, or someone might prefer to extend a summer vacation rather than celebrate Columbus Day.) Doing this provides the company with some operational flexibility. Your offices and stores can stay open throughout the year, staffed by people who have no objection to working on a specific holiday.

Sick leave. Most companies provide for these with specific plans varying widely. On average, nine sick days are awarded each year.

Jury duty. All states have laws requiring employers to grant time off for jury duty, but most do not require the employer to compensate the employee for jury duty. This places an incredible burden on the employee, since some jurisdictions pay as little as $5 a day to the jurors.

You can demonstrate your community commitment, as well as do the right thing, by paying employees their full salaries, as well as allowing them to keep compensation paid by the court. This is a little thing, to be sure, but worker loyalty is often made up of a collection of small acts.

Retirement vehicle. Retirement plans are excellent retention tools for many reasons. For instance, vesting periods can run for as long as five years, and the employee must stay to reap the benefits.

There is another retention benefit to having excellent retirement benefits. It sets up an expectation that you fully expect employees to stay with you until they retire. It makes a bold statement about your relationship. Retirement plans promote a stable workforce.

Other insurance. Benefits packages often include life insurance, short- and long-term disability insurance, as well as dental and vision plans. Since most of the costs for these plans can be passed on to the worker, it makes sense to include these protections in your packages.

Educational assistance. By reimbursing people for their education you reap two benefits. Someone else is training your workers a whole lot cheaper than you can do it for, and employees think you are a benevolent company for paying for their education. Why wouldn't a company offer this benefit?

Credit union membership. These relationships are easy to establish, cost the company nothing, yet deliver strong benefits to the employees.

Merchant discounts. With a little effort, you can provide a visible and fun set of benefits with a merchant discount program. Basically, you form a cooperative with other businesses to offer each other's employees the same discount they provide their own workers. Amusement parks, restaurants, and local movie theatres are also willing to provide discounts to your people. Here is another benefit that costs you nothing yet provides good benefits to your employees.

Best **Tip**
Create a nice benefit by joining with other businesses to give employees of all participating companies discounts.

Which of these benefits should you offer? When designing your benefit package, just remember this. You don't need to give your employees everything they want. You just need to give them more than the competition is giving.

Employees' Favorite 'New' Perks

To get bang for your bucks, you should offer new benefits that have the most meaning to your employees. Here are some perks that are rated most highly by American workers. In other words, if you offer them, you will get an extremely positive response from your workers.

- On-site child care
- Free lunch

- Personal concierge service
- Dry cleaning service
- Home-purchasing services
- Adoption aid
- Subsidized cafeterias
- On-site ATM
- Personal travel service
- Elder-care resource or referral
- Casual dress every day

Now, let me make a little prediction. As you were reading this list, the hair began to stand up on the back of your neck. You may have been saying to yourself, *Concierge services? Free lunch? The nerve of these people! Next they'll want me to hand-feed them peeled grapes!*

I understand the reaction. It may appear that those taking this survey were trying to leverage some silly extras, but that's not really the case. Underlying the request for these "perks" is really an appeal for you to help them offset personal obligations they have that sometime interfere with their work.

For instance, how often are your workers late or absent because of childcare problems? You can solve this business problem by solving a personal problem. Offer on-site childcare facilities and absenteeism will plummet. (You can pass on some or most of the costs on to your employees and still receive kudos from you people. They, too, are seeking a solution to their attendance problems.) Many companies offer free lunches because by doing so people don't leave the premises for lunch and they return to work sooner. Look at other "requests" on the list. Consider how your business would benefit by providing these perks.

Best Tip

Helping employees solve problems like obtaining child care can help you solve problems with absenteeism.

Small Company, Big Benefits

You may be reading this chapter and thinking, *That's great advice for General Motors, but I run a five-person company. I can't get benefits like that!* I have good news for you: Yes you can.

You are able to get full benefits for every member of your organization. And, these benefits will be as good—if not better—than those offered by huge corporations.

The route to these benefits is called a PEO, which stands for Professional Employer Organization. This industry was formed to specifically address the issue of providing benefits and services to the small business. PEOs are a co-employment relationship. Under the eyes of the law, your employees become the PEO's employees for certain matters such as payroll and tax purposes. For benefit purposes, your workers are no longer the employees of a five-man company, they are part of a *20,000*-employee company. They now become eligible for a benefit package befitting a giant corporation. The quality of these benefits is as good as it gets and the cost is reasonable.

Best Tip

Give your employees big-company benefits by hooking up with a Professional Employer Organization.

There are many more aspects to a PEO relationship, including payroll, tax services, training in certain areas, and more. I encourage you to explore this option not only for the benefits to your employees but the benefit to your company as well. Look in the yellow pages under *Professional Employer Organizations* and invite a few companies to come out and speak with you.

Take the Credit

Our discussion of benefits noted that while these benefits may be worth as much as a third of the total compensation package, most workers take them for granted. Don't let your benefit pack-

---

RETENTION IN ACTION: THE CONTAINER STORE

When Kip Tindell co-founded The Container Store, he was determined that its employees would be the best paid in the retail industry. Indeed, salaries are *50 to 100 percent higher* than other stores. In addition, it offers a benefits package that no other organization can come close to.

Tindell declared, "If you believe that one great person is worth three good people in terms of business productivity, it makes sense to pay somebody twice what other companies would."

Tindell goes on to make his business case: "The company wins because it is getting three times the productivity at two times the cost." The Container Store's turnover rate runs 15 to 25 percent. The retail industry averages more than 100 percent turnover.

---

age go unnoticed. Take credit for these perks.

Discuss the benefits in detail when making the salary offer and again at each annual performance review. Let the employee know their dollar value. Both you and the employee will be amazed at the value that these benefits provide and the cost to the company for providing them.

Job Security

You cannot fully appreciate a human being's need for security until you ponder the fact that kamikaze pilots wore crash helmets.

There was once an unofficial contract between worker and company. Employees promised to work hard, give their best efforts, and be loyal to the company. The company provided a job for life, regular salary increases, career growth, and identity.

While this contract may seem hopelessly outdated in the age of managed layoffs and worker free agency, it served America well for most of the twentieth century. It made possible the thirty-year mortgages and college educations that the American Dream is made of. The higher one climbed in a company, the greater the rewards and the stronger the incentive to stick around.

Ten million layoffs later, the contract is but a rotting corpse. And companies are scratching their heads trying to uncover the secret of retaining workers and cultivating their loyalty. They need only look at history. Responsible employers take a long view of employment. They use layoffs as a last resort and offer a concept known as Lifetime Employment. This concept does not imply that they disregard shareholders, guarantee jobs for life, or retain workers who perform poorly. Rather it means that the company operates with the *intent* of providing a position and growth opportunities that would sustain an employee's entire career.

No one faults a company for laying off workers when the company's actual existence is in jeopardy. The problem lies in using massive layoffs as a quick-fix for shoring up stock values. Wall Street rewards companies that kick out thousands of workers by increasing (temporarily) the price of the stock. Notice how often massive layoffs occur just before stockholders' meetings?

The odd thing about these layoffs is that the company often ends the year with the same number of employees that they started with before the layoffs. It was a gimmick to drive stock prices. So what is the harm? Have we forgotten about the effect on the workers including those who were not laid off? When a company labels its people as just another asset, people feel as if they are nothing more than a piece of disposable equipment. And it is these same companies that scratch their heads and wonder why people are not loyal the way they were in the old days.

Be Wary of Reorganizations

The relatively new procedure of routinely adjusting a company's organizational structure is a cultural issue, not a management one. *If it ain't broken, break it!* was a recent management guru rallying cry (and book title). I am envious of the number of books it sold, but I'm infuriated at the author-guru for the devastating effect it had on companies and the lives of their employees.

Companies do need to change their structure from time to time. This is usually due to growth or the entry/exit into new industries or territories. Business has an obligation to adjust to these conditions. But these situations are not what I am addressing. I am addressing the use of reorganizations as a management experiment, or to cover up problems in the company, or to simply get attention by playing the business game in a clever manner.

Business is not a game. Stockholders' investments are not personal toys. Employees are not inanimate chess pieces. If you create a culture of instability, good people will look elsewhere for their careers to flourish. Not one quality person—*not one*—will put up with a company playing games with his or her livelihood. The only people who will stay with you are those too insecure in themselves to seek a more reasonable employer. If you play this hideous game, your company will eventually be composed of insecure and mediocre people.

I doubt many CEOs of *Fortune* 500 companies are reading my words. But I do think a lot of *future* CEOs are. And it is to you I say, *Do not play this destructive game of self-mutilation.* It solves nothing and will wreak terror in the company you have been given stewardship over.

Training

When you buy a new machine, you immediately ask: How do I get the most out of this machine? How do I repair it? What maintenance schedule do I set up if I want to get a good return on my investment? These are the same questions that should be asked when hiring a new worker.

You may think that training is a subject better dealt with in chapter seven, personal fulfillment. But I am not talking about career-development or job-enrichment training right now. I am addressing the basic indoctrination that each worker needs to perform his job confidently. This type of training is considered more of a job-security issue rather than as a career enrichment subject.

You may be surprised at how many workers are thrown into the lake and told to swim. They are expected to learn their responsibilities through osmosis and immediately perform credibly. And it is not just at the entry-level that we see this. Staff positions are often treated this way. After all, if he was an accountant for another company, then why can't he immediately function as an accountant here?

People will quit when they feel insecure and unconfident. You must provide the basics as well as an adjustment period to *every* new employee.

According to the *Harvard Business Review,* the biggest reason for employee turnover among Gen X workers is lack of training. While I cannot agree that this is the *top* reason, the desire to learn is a significant catalyst in the attraction and retention of these younger workers. If employees are going to make a commitment to an employer today, they want to know what kind of commitment the employer is going to make to them.

Invest in your people by providing development opportunities for them. Are you afraid you'll lose them if they broaden their capabilities? You might. A valid fear is, *What if I train them and they leave?* To me, though, a scarier question is, *What if I don't train them and they stay?*

Safety

This section does not refer to the things overseen by OSHA. Those issues are well addressed by government authorities and insurance providers. Sadly, our safety discussion must be about workplace violence.

Workplace violence is not new, but it now seems to be commonplace as opposed to its previous novelty. The workplace reflects society and society is increasingly using violent means to

RETENTION IN ACTION: MALDEN MILLS

You probably don't recognize the name of this company, but you may recall the attention it received in the mid 1990s. Just before Christmas, a fire destroyed this clothing mill, which made Polartec fleece, in Lawrence, Massachusetts. The mill was fully covered by insurance and its owner, Aaron Feuerstein, was at an age where most people considered retirement.

The thousand workers and the city that depended on the payroll braced itself for financial disaster. Even if the mill were rebuilt, it would be a long time before it was operating again. They all mourned their loss as they assembled for an announcement from Feuerstein. All assumed he would thank them for their service and wish them well.

The first shock came as he declared that the plant would be rebuilt. And then he completely caught them off-guard announcing that every one of the thousand workers would be kept on the payroll—with full benefits—until the mill could be reopened.

The immediate reaction to this announcement was enthusiastic. Every newspaper, TV station, and magazine in the country declared its personal admiration. The president invited Feuerstein to the State of the Union address, and labor unions made him a poster boy for compassionate management.

But all this publicity was based on misunderstanding what was really driving Feuerstein's decision-making process. Some people assumed he acted selflessly and benevolently, even against his own best interests. They were wrong.

Then again, other people called him a self-promoter and a publicity hound. They felt he was just an old man who wanted the attraction of the lights and cameras, reveling in the public adoration. Many business experts declared him a fool for risking the continued existence of his company just so he could bask in glory. They argued that he should have not paid out $15 million in wages and benefits to workers when they no longer had a place to work. They further declared that he owed it to his business to relocate the mill somewhere labor was cheaper, like in the South or overseas.

So, which was it? Was Feuerstein a saint or a fool? Neither. He was a smart, efficient businessman. He honestly believed the cliché, *Our people are our greatest asset.*

Feuerstein responds to his critics: "Why would I go to Thailand to bring the cost lower when I might run the risk of losing the advantage I've got, which is superior quality?" And to get that quality, he worked hard for decades to build a powerful team. The correlation between loyal customers and loyal employees is no coincidence and he did not want to lose an incredible asset that had taken him decades to develop.

Even before the fire, turnover ran below five percent. Productivity? From 1982 to 1995, revenues tripled while the work force only doubled. Aaron Feuerstein is not a fool. He is not a saint. He is a good businessman.

express frustrations. Indeed, who could have anticipated that the phrase *going postal* would become part of our business vocabulary?

While you cannot ensure that violence will never occur in your workplace, there are some things you can do to promote safety.

- **Do not tolerate joking about violence.** The airports have it right; take all statements seriously. Make it clear that jokes about violence will not be taken lightly and such comments are completely out of bounds. "I was just joking," does not hold up in sexual harassment suits and it should have equal validity when it comes to violence.

- **Do not accept any acts of violence.** Horseplay may begin as fun but often turns quite serious. Have strict policies on "small" acts of violence, such as shoving. Mild violence can often be an indication of major problems. Deal with borderline cases as you would an assault.

- **Do not allow threatening behavior.** Although we think of the word assault as referring to a violent action, it really means threatening to harm. The point is that threatening is just as bad as committing the act physically. Threatening words usually precede violent acts. Make it clear that you will not tolerate your employees being threatened or intimidated in any way.

- **Ban all weapons.** Your policy should forbid weapons not only in the workplace but also in the parking lot. What is a weapon? The best definition I have come up with is this: If you can't take it aboard an airplane, you can't bring it on company property.

- **Follow security measures strictly.** Emphasize to your employees that you have put security measures into place for their protection. They should not try to beat the system. Propping doors open, exiting through the back door, or allowing access to someone without a proper ID are all actions that have lead to people being killed.

- **Train your employees how to respond to violence.** It happens. And we should do all we can to ensure our people know how to deal with these situations. Managers should know how to defuse hostile situations. Workers should know how to react to robberies.

People will work in an environment of fear only until they can find a safer place to work. It is one of the core basics in the hierarchy of needs. Conversely, a safe atmosphere encourages retention. Do not overlook this issue when developing your retention plan.

The Agile Manager's Checklist

✔ To keep retention high, while still maintaining fiscal responsibility, pay in the 75th percentile for your industry.

✔ If you have any hope of attracting a quality workforce, provide paid medical insurance.

✔ You don't need to give employees everything they want—just more than your competitors do.

✔ Make sure employees know exactly what your benefits package is worth to them.

✔ Gen Xers, more than any other generational group, want the opportunity to learn new skills.

Chapter Six

Relationships with Managers and Co-Workers

"I will pay more for the ability to deal with people than any other ability under the sun."

—JOHN D. ROCKEFELLER

"Well, I guess I haven't been this happy for four years," said Scott. Not coincidentally, Scott had been promoted to sales manager four years earlier. But two months ago, the Agile Manager had returned him to the sales force, no longer a manager. And, more importantly, no longer the greatest single source of employee attrition since General George Custer.

"So, it's working out well for you?" the Agile Manager asked, rhetorically. He had to admit, once Scott had management responsibility removed from him, he was a rather enjoyable person to talk with. Perhaps that was what got him promoted to start with. But now he was back in his real profession and leading the company in sales for the second straight month.

Scott beamed as he recounted the past few weeks. It had been a shock when he was first told that he could either take a severance package or return to the trenches. In fact, he made several ear-reddening remarks, including a few personal swipes at the Agile Manager. "But once I really thought about it, I realized that I wasn't made to be a manager. I hated being the boss. And I was a horrible manager. But, you know what? I'm a great salesman."

"That you are," the Agile Manager agreed. He was enjoying the real progress that had occurred recently. Scott had been replaced by an external hire who had immediately bonded with the salesforce. He was taking care of his people and they were all producing. And, it seemed, they were all staying with the company, at least for the near future.

We'll call this a "win," the Agile Manager noted to himself.

I was chatting with an old friend who just happens to be a compensation analyst with FedEx. It is Ken Elliott's job to assure that all the company's pay rates are competitive with the marketplace. He dedicates his time to the study of compensation and its effect on attracting and maintaining a great workforce. He seemed to be the ideal person to get information for the compensation section of this book.

I asked him my standard lead-in question, "What have you found to be the most critical thing in employee retention?" He didn't hesitate with his answer. "Well, it's pretty much like this. If they like their boss they stay. If they don't like him they quit."

Indeed. The funny thing is, that is pretty much the response I got from every company I spoke with. I decided that I could sum up the subject of retention with *If they like their boss they stay. If they don't like him they quit.* Now all I needed to do was add 30,000 adverbs and submit it to my publisher.

The Value of Good Management

People join companies and leave managers. A Gallup poll underscored this by noting that employees with "lousy" managers are four times more likely to quit than those with "nice" managers. Yet, if you look at exit interviews, this rarely is stated as a reason. In fact, if you were to ask most employers to name the primary reason people quit, I doubt any of them would point to themselves.

When you ask managers to diagnose the reasons employees quit, they invariably point to a variety of external factors, including money, better opportunities, or long hours. They fail to take any personal responsibility for the situation. But the fact is that most of the problems causing turnover are completely within the manager's control! Bottom line: The biggest cause of turnover is incompetent managers with poor skills in human relations.

Recognize Poor Management

Hire supervisors with excellent people skills. Good supervisors know how to build trust with their people. They are great communicators, are open and able to take personal criticism. They give recognition liberally and help their people achieve their goals. They are rewarded for their skills by having loyal, energetic, productive people who stay with the company.

But even well-run organizations sometimes have a pocket with unusually high turnover, low productivity, and miserable morale. Pay attention to those pockets.

Here's how you can spot those with poor people-management skills:

"**Bad morale.**" A poor people manager spends a lot of time complaining about the quality and morale of his people. They are never good enough, and he will emphasize how work ethics "have really slipped in this new generation." He always has a hard time finding "good employees." No matter who he brings in, they're never acceptable.

> **Best Tip**
>
> Deal with poor managers *now*. They are your greatest impediment to keeping good people on staff.

Offloads responsibility. Further, rather than hiring talented people and then developing their skills, he's expecting the HR department to furnish him "off-the-rack" workers in which he won't have to invest any personal equity.

RETENTION IN ACTION: FEDEX

Management is rarely awarded the same status as other disciplines such as finance, legal, or marketing. How often is the best salesman made the sales manager—with disastrous results? Some companies are so blasé about putting people into management that there is almost an attitude of "anyone can be a manager." Perhaps that is why there are so many poor managers with wretched people skills.

It doesn't happen that way at FedEx. Promotion into management involves programs designed to question whether or not someone is cut out to be a manager or if management is really the right thing for him or her. This begins with an interesting acronym, LEAP, the Leadership Evaluation Awareness Process. This program encourages management applicants (both internal and external) to examine their desires and aptitudes for becoming managers.

LEAP begins with a class called, "Is Management for Me?" It details the nature of management positions and challenges applicants to examine whether they truly want to become managers. This class is followed by individually tailored self-study and awareness-building activities, designed to further examine a person's suitability for management.

LEAP continues with the requirement to obtain management recommendations, extensive peer assessments and, finally, a panel evaluation.

This is an exhaustive and thorough screening, to be sure. But it has been effective in encouraging successful transitions from worker to manager. In the twenty months before the introduction of LEAP, 10.7 percent of new managers who entered the system left within that same twenty-month period. In LEAP's first twenty months of existence, only 1.7 percent of LEAP-endorsed managers left within that twenty-month timeframe.

More transfers out than in. Also, people refuse to transfer into a poor manager's department, but there are frequent requests for transfers out. As a result, his department is drained of experienced workers and becomes a depository for employees that are new to the company.

Many grievances. Workers frequently complain about the poor manager of people, and he is the subject of a disproportionate share of union grievances. Performance reviews are regularly challenged.

I don't want to be guilty of using circular logic, but the easiest way to identify a poor manager is to see a high attrition rate.

Bottom line: Identify your poor managers and either teach them how to manage people or get them out of your system. Poor managers are killing your retention. There is nothing you can do that will have a greater impact on retention than ensuring all of your employees are served by someone with solid people skills.

The Workplace: America's New Community

At one time in America, *community* was defined as a place where we lived. Our neighborhood, the people who lived next door, and our local schools defined our community. But this has changed. Today the new community is the workplace. We now look to our jobs for support we once looked for in our neighborhoods. Retention strategies must incorporate community-type services to meet the needs of today's workers.

Many companies recognize this and engineer programs to foster a sense of community. These programs run the gamut from softball teams and bowling leagues to picnics and banquets.

Labor unions are particularly good at seizing this opportunity to build member loyalty. They actively arrange for group recreation and actually strengthen their grip on the workforce in this way. Indeed, by having many "family" activities for their members, unions are able to generate a feeling of loyalty toward them, rather than for the company.

Take full advantage of developing social and recreational opportunities for your employees. Little involvement is required by management to make these things happen. This is because there are natural organizers and cheerleaders in your workforce already, eagerly awaiting your permission to be unleashed. Simply give them the tools to develop programs and watch the community flourish. Let groups use company facilities to meet to arrange for parties and activities. Include announcements in the company newsletter. Provide seed money for the purchase of equipment and supplies. But the leadership for such activities will come from eager volunteers. Your people want to develop a family relationship with your company. All you have to do is give them minimal support and they'll run with it.

> **Best Tip**
>
> Strive to create a sense of community at your workplace. If you don't, you may end up watching a union do it for you.

Provide a Family Friendly Culture

Despite the significant role that work now plays in the lives of our employees, people demand a balance. More time is needed for the family and their personal lives. Although it may sound like a paradox, people turn to their work for ways to expand their personal lives.

You should explore ways your company can address this employee need. Here are some ideas that do this. At the same time, they may actually give your company greater productivity and flexibility.

Provide a buffet of valuable work/life programs. There are many ways to make day-to-day life easier for employees. Consider some of these: on-site childcare, parenting courses, elder care; adoption aid; scholarship programs; and referrals for such things as tutors, home health organizations, legal services, and counseling for various personal issues.

While these programs are not traditional benefits that companies usually offer, studies show that employees with access to these types of benefits have the best performance appraisal ratings. These employees also express an intention to remain with the company for the long haul. Today's employees are generally overburdened and looking for assistance. A company reaps *tremendous* payback in loyalty and appreciation when it solves employees' personal issues.

Adopt a flexible scheduling policy. This is just about the easiest and least expensive family-friendly policy to adopt. Not only does flexible scheduling send the message that you care about an employee's need to balance work and personal time, but you usually end up with a more efficient office. Flexible scheduling can take several forms. One of the most popular is flextime, where employees work when they choose, as long as they put in a specified amount of hours in a given period. Employees are required to be in the office during a specific core time, such as from 10 A.M. to 2 P.M., but they are allowed to schedule their start and end times around those hours.

Job sharing. This has become a popular option for many mothers who want to continue their careers on a part-time basis. Basically, a single job is split between two people. This situation adapts itself best to secretarial, production, or administrative jobs, but has also been known to work in creative and policy-making positions.

The worker benefits because she is able to have both a career and a family. The company benefits because it now has two highly motivated people for a single job. Job sharing also eliminates those problems caused by covering for illnesses and vacations. Overtime is minimized, as are expenses for temp services during particularly busy times. (For instance, both workers may work full time during the busy Christmas season.)

Explore the uncharted world of telecommuting. Mapmakers during the fifteenth century had a clever way of dealing with lands they didn't know much about. They would simply make the notation: *Here there be dragons.* I want to mark this section with the same caveat. Telecommuting may be a godsend for a lot of workers.

Then again, some employees will destroy their careers because of their inability to navigate these unknown waters.

That said, employees with high motivation, self-discipline, necessary skills, and independent orientation are ideal candidates to work from their homes. Telecommuting may be used as a permanent arrangement, thus providing you with significant savings in office expenses, or it may be used for parts of the week, such as Mondays or Fridays. Telecommuting will build loyalty and productivity in many cases, but choose your workers carefully. Successful telecommuting requires tremendous discipline and few people are good candidates for this arrangement.

- Do not permit telecommuting if the employee says she wants to work at home to better look after her children. You cannot work at home or anywhere else and supervise children at the same time.

- Carefully measure production, especially during the first few months. Set specific short-term goals so you can gauge employee performance at home. Does the worker maintain his previous levels of quality, timeliness, and production?

Family-Friendly Policies in Action

Let's look at some real-life examples of companies offering creative family-friendly policies that make a huge impact on their employees' morale.

One fear that many workers have is that their careers will suffer if they take advantage of the family-friendly policies. After all, there remains an old-school culture in many companies that says you really aren't part of the team unless you dedicate all of your waking hours to the company. Deloitte & Touche, one of the nation's top accounting firms, is one starched-shirt company that refuses to let that attitude be a part of its culture. It allows their professionals to work reduced schedules while remaining on the partnership track. Fewer than 5 percent of its accountants choose this option. Offering this program has, however, dramatically lowered turnover, especially among women.

Ohio-based Dawson Personnel Systems listened to its employees and heard their needs expressed clearly. They wanted more time with their families. So management experimented and wanted to see what would happen if they offered employees generous amounts of time off once their jobs were completed. The first trial was with the sales force. Individual productivity goals for the new year were set 20 percent higher than the previous year. That action caused the rumblings of a mutiny until the company offered an incentive. They were told that once they met their monthly goals, they could go home at two o'clock the rest of the month. This program was an enormous success. The sales force is spending more time with its families and making huge sales commissions. And the company has experienced a record-breaking sales increase. Everybody wins.

If you travel a great deal, you know just how hard it is to have a normal family life. Workers at Andersen Consulting have to endure a tremendous amount of travel in performing their duties, but the company has adopted a policy that helps relieve some of the stress. The company applies what it calls a *seven to seven* travel policy. No one is required to leave home any earlier than 7:00 A.M. on Monday and all employees are expected to return back home by 7:00 P.M. on Friday. For the heavy traveler, this policy opens up a lot of dependable quality time with their families in a world that usually ignores this need.

Best Tip

Shed the idea that employees must devote every waking hour to your company. Many organizations have—and prospered.

And finally, consider the actions of the Plitt Company, a Chicago seafood business. Two weekends a year, the company throws a party for the employees' children in order to celebrate their academic achievements. The children are awarded up to $20 for each *A* they've earned in school. Many companies sponsor programs, such as this one, to call attention to the accomplishments

RETENTION IN ACTION: CHICK-FIL-A

Chick-fil-A sells chicken sandwiches, waffle fries, chicken nuggets, and other related products. This rapidly growing fast-food chain has almost a thousand restaurants in thirty-two states. While one could argue that it serves food of exceptionally high quality and that its marketing is quite clever (featuring cows begging for their lives by asking that we all *Eat Mor Chikin*), it is the employee-focused culture that truly distinguishes this company.

Chick-fil-A's retention rates will appear to be a misprint. Among its operators (restaurant managers), it has an annual attrition rate of about 3 percent—3 percent! If you subtract deaths and retirement, there is not a whole lot of room for resignations. Further, its turnover among hourly crew is about a third that of other restaurant companies. How is this possible?

Chick-fil-A's retention begins with the selection process. It is not easy to become part of the Chick-fil-A family. In a recent year, about ten thousand applications were received for the sixty or so restaurant manager positions made available by new store openings. An additional five thousand applications were submitted for the sixty new positions at their corporate headquarters. "We date people for a long time before we marry them," says Andy Lorenzen, senior consultant for Team Retention and People Development. (If ever there was a need for an acronym . . .) "We believe there must be a match between character, competence and chemistry." And the company takes its time, conducting countless interviews to ensure that the relationship will endure a long time. It can literally take years to become a Chick-fil-A operator.

Once the company has hired someone, it takes its responsibilities toward him or her seriously. "People work for a person, not a brand," Lorenzen adds. "If you ask most of our people who they work for, they name their boss, not Chick-fil-A." So the company encourages that relationship. For instance, it honors personal family time, as well as employees' responsibilities to their religious organizations and communities.

This honoring of personal needs and responsibilities is dramatically demonstrated by more than a lot of talk. Consider this: The majority of its restaurants are located in shopping malls. Sunday is the biggest traffic day in most of these malls. Even so, every restaurant is closed on Sunday. Its culture says that family time is its priority; Chick-fil-A walks its talk.

of workers' children. Don't take such fun and inexpensive programs lightly. You will build tremendous employee loyalty any time you pay attention to the employees' families, particularly their children.

Here is my favorite story about a company that includes employee families as an important part of its culture. FedEx holds a lottery whenever the company purchases a new airplane. The prize? The winner has his or her child's name put on the new airplane. Can you imagine the emotional rush of seeing a DC-10 named after your daughter? Now, you probably don't have any aircraft sitting around awaiting a name, but I'll bet that if you thought about it a bit you could find a way to apply a similar program to your company or department.

Tackle Harassment

There is a viper that could be in your organization that will kill all teamwork and sense of community. The subject of harassment has been preached and laws enforced for the past two decades. Fortunately, laws are strict and punishment severe for anyone who creates a workplace that includes sexual or racial harassment.

There is little I can add to this subject except to underscore that you must stamp out any form of harassment and discrimination in your workplace. And legal liability isn't your chief concern—harassment is a poison that will destroy your team and result in ferocious attrition.

I also want to address a more sinister form of harassment. It is a behavior that is often overlooked by management yet results in more turnover than any of the illegal forms of harassment. The poison is known by an innocent, almost adolescent, term—bullying.

Bullying is basically harassment between peers. It manifests itself quietly—often behind closed doors—but devastates its victims, who are often embarrassed to report the problem. A bully will lie, make veiled or not-so-veiled threats, and in general make life miserable for his or her prey.

This is an area that human resource managers have failed to address. In many companies, as long as an employee continues to get results, he or she will face no adverse consequences for bullying other employees. This approach is short sighted, as decreased morale and heavy turnover is the inevitable result.

Am I overplaying this problem? Look at some statistics. The University of North Carolina conducted a survey among 775 people who said they had been treated rudely or disrespectfully at work. The study found:

- Fifty-three percent lost work time worrying about the incident or future interactions.
- Twenty-eight percent lost work time avoiding the bully.
- Ten percent worked fewer hours.
- Twelve percent actually changed jobs just to avoid the bully.

These are *huge* numbers with a devastating impact on your team.

Lower productivity, absenteeism, and dramatically increased turn-over are expensive and significant situations. Employee satisfaction surveys consistently find that the way people are treated at work is in direct correlation to employee satisfaction. Employees who feel they are not treated respectfully are much more likely than average to resign within a year. This situation cannot be treated lightly.

Deal with bullying firmly. Here are some suggestions on how you can become involved to ensure that you have a harassment-free workplace.

- Explain to your workforce what bullying is and the firm actions you will take if such behavior occurs.
- Make certain your managers understand how serious this problem really is. Never downplay an employee's complaint that he is being bullied. Psychological injuries are just as serious as physical ones.
- Have outlets in place so that bullying can be uncovered. Employee hotlines, suggestion boxes, and culture surveys are effective tools, but the most effective might be for your managers to be aware of the potential problem and they keep their ears open for signs of trouble.
- Management should take responsibility for solving the problem. Do not expect the employee to confront the bully alone. There wouldn't be a problem if he were able to do this in the first place.
- Immediately separate the target from the bully. This is especially important, because bullies generally retaliate. If you cannot transfer the victim, consider placing him on paid leave until the problem is solved.
- Consider sacrificing a bully or two, even if they are top performers, to prove to your employees that you're serious about curtailing these harmful tactics.

Here is the bright side: While this is a major cause of attrition, the solution does not require any large expenditures of money. You can have a solid impact on your turnover problem without having to request any funding.

The Agile Manager's Checklist

✔ The biggest cause of turnover is incompetent managers with poor skills in human relations.

✔ Given that fact, hire only managers with good people skills.

✔ Foster a sense of community by fielding a softball or bowling team, or by holding regular social events.

✔ Try flexible scheduling. It's one of your strongest weapons in combatting turnover.

✔ Root out any form of harassment in your company before it destroys you.

Chapter Seven

*E*nable Personal Fulfillment

"Do you single out individuals for public praise and recognition? Make people who work for you feel important. If you honor and serve them, they'll honor and serve you."

—MARY KAY ASH, FOUNDER, MARY KAY COSMETICS

"Outstanding leaders go out of their way to boost the self-esteem of their personnel. If people believe in themselves, it's amazing what they can accomplish."

—SAM WALTON

"And finally, I met with Katherine and showed her the status of all the dangling issues. It's not exactly in her job description, but I thought that it would be good for her to be exposed to some new departments." The Agile Manager had returned from his assignment with the merged company. Although he would continue to monitor things by phone, his day-to-day work had ended. He was

giving his boss a verbal report on the project.

"That was smart," Jim replied. "It's important to occasionally give people challenging assignments in somewhat unfamiliar areas. It keeps their jobs interesting and helps their career development."

The Agile Manager was suddenly hit with a revelation. "So that's why you had me do this project," he said. "You wanted to give me an assignment that would expand my horizons. Jim, you were developing me."

"To a great degree, yes," replied Jim. "You are one of the most valuable people in this company and I certainly did want you to have the opportunity to learn some new things. And, I wanted to see how your staff would handle their additional responsibilities while you were away. But the main reason for this assignment was self-evident. We had a monstrous problem over there. I needed it solved. You did. And no one is surprised."

The Agile Manager couldn't suppress the smile that spread from ear to ear. It was quite an explosion of compliments, he realized. His boss had, in just a couple of sentences, evaluated his performance, explained the assignment and motivated him to a higher degree than anyone had ever done inside sixty seconds.

The Agile Manager thought to himself: "Wow, he's good."

The executive began the meeting by reviewing the company's latest corporate strategic plan. "You know how we have always said, *Our people are our greatest asset*? Well, we have re-evaluated our priorities. Cash. Cash is now considered our number one asset."

"Where do *people* rank now?" a salesman asked.

"Sixteenth. Right after coffee filters."

We have seen the workplace evolve from simply a place to earn money into one that attempts to provide all human need. This is not really a stretch of logic, mind you. Since the average executive spends more time with his job than his family, it is no wonder that he looks to work to satisfy most of his desires.

Nowhere is that more apparent than in a person's need for personal fulfillment. Notice what happens when a man is introduced.

What is he asked right after he gives his name? That's right, the inevitable question is, "What do you do?" Work supplies many people's identity, so it is reasonable that those same people look to the workplace to absorb a sense of value. Let's explore ways the company can provide for this need and thus increase its chance to retain these achievement-minded workers.

Create a Sense of Personal Value

A friend once said to me, "You know, if I had a nickel for every time a boss has told me I was appreciated, well, I guess I would have a dime." I feel pity for this man, because I have been quite fortunate to be exposed to some great, inspirational leaders in my career.

Perhaps the best motivator I have known is Clint Clark. He was serving as the president of a company in which I was a regional VP. I was based in another state and arrived completely unannounced at the corporate office one day. Just as I entered the building, I

> ### Best Tip
>
> Praise people often. Most managers do a very poor job showing appreciation for their employees.

came face to face with Clint. He stopped and was momentarily surprised. But without missing a beat, Clint handed me a small lapel pin that read, *Customer Service is #1.*

"Ken, I've been looking for you," he said. "I want you to have this, because I don't know anyone who cares more about customer service than you." I was about to burst with pride; I've never had anyone say anything so motivating to me in my life. And this was being said by the president!

Of course, it probably would have meant even more if it were not for the fact that he was holding a box of about a thousand of those lapel pins. OK, so he was BS-ing me. But that's not the point. I was motivated because Clint was *taking the trouble* to snow me.

I saw this exact principle in action some time later. I was visiting one of our stores. I had not been in the facility in several months and was absolutely amazed at how improved it was. The manager gave me a store tour and I let him brag on himself a while. Then I turned to him, took that pin off my jacket and placed it on his shirt. "Here, " I said. "Clint gave me this personally. But I am so proud of what you have done here that I want you to have it."

Several years later, when I had been long gone from that company, I happened to visit that store as a customer. That same manager was there. And you know what? He was wearing that pin. Simple acts of appreciation cost nothing but get big results that last a long time.

Best Tip

To show appreciation, take an employee to lunch. Even better, invite his or her spouse to come, too.

Wichita State University did a study of 1,500 employees on the subject of motivation. This study found that the most powerful motivator was having the boss personally congratulate the person on a job well done. This tool is without any cost whatsoever. Yet this same study found that only 42 percent of these participants were recognized by their company in this manner.

Here we have a near-perfect business tool. Letting your employees know that you value them costs little and in some cases nothing at all. Yet it has a dramatic impact on retention. Why don't we use it more? Perhaps we cannot think of ways to do it.

Here's a list of low-cost, effective ways to let your employees know that you appreciate them. Use it and reap the financial windfall.

- Call an employee into your office just to say thanks. Don't discuss any other issue during the visit.
- Give him a day off. Better yet, make it a three-day weekend.
- Take her and her spouse to lunch.

- Community newspapers are on the constant lookout for editorial material. Send them a news release about one of your employees and they will almost certainly print it.
- Bake her a batch of cookies.
- Give him a couple of movie tickets for a weekday afternoon matinee.
- Send her an e-mail expressing your appreciation. Then cc everyone in the company.
- Provide a gift certificate to a restaurant.
- Write a letter to the employee's family telling it about a recent accomplishment of the employee and what it means to you and the company.
- Do his least favorite task for a week.
- Purchase one of those electronic scrolling marquees and put it in your work area. Place a congratulatory message on it so that he sees his name and accomplishment in lights.
- Give her a leather notebook with the company logo.
- Create a lapel pin.
- Write a letter of commendation and place a copy in his file.
- Publicize employee achievements in newsletters.
- Arrange for the CEO to have a recognition lunch with the employee.
- Dedicate the parking space closest to the building entrance for the outstanding employee of the month.
- Wash her car in the parking lot during lunch one day.
- Personally make breakfast for your team upon the achievement of a goal.
- Use employees in your company commercials, even if it is just a "walk-on" role. Not on TV? Use their pictures in print ads.
- Celebrate tenure! If you honestly believe that retention is important, make a huge deal out of anniversary dates. Parties. Awards. Gifts. Banners. Nothing is too bold to declare your

excitement and appreciation for an employee's longevity.

■ Unquestionably, the best way to let an employee know she is appreciated is also the least expensive. Nothing, *and I do mean nothing*, has a greater impact than regularly looking the employee in the eye and saying, "thank you."

There are probably a few blank pages somewhere in this book. Pretend that we did that on purpose and use them to keep a running list of ideas for showing your people how much you value them.

Schedule Spontaneity

How can you assure yourself that you make spontaneous compliments to your employees? Schedule them. In fact, let's do this right now. Pull out your daily planner. Write down the name of an employee for each week. During each employee's week, be on the constant lookout for that person to do something noteworthy. (Don't worry, if you look for something, you'll find lots of opportunities.) When you catch the person-of-the-week doing something noteworthy, lavish her with praise.

And, while you are at it, schedule some times to display public acts of affection. Here's an example of what I mean. I have a friend who runs a small interior decorating firm. She makes maximum use of the company's voice mail system to communicate with all the employees, so they are in the habit to check her messages and "updates" each morning.

Apparently, she even leaves messages on holidays. One Thanksgiving morning, the employees awoke to this message:

> I am counting my blessings today, and I wanted you to know how much I appreciate having you working with me. I am truly blessed to have a company with such talented, professional people.

You can phrase your comments to fit your style and you can decide between voicemail, memo, or e-mail. But go ahead and mark three or four days on your calendar during the next year in which you will make a public display of affection. In fact, go ahead and compose the message now so that when the time comes you can easily send it out.

Promote Peer Recognition

Do not underestimate the power of peer recognition. It is powerful and management should find ways to encourage it. AT&T Universal Card Services in Jacksonville, Florida, furnishes its employees with a pad of colored paper shaped like a globe with "Thank You" written all over it in different languages. Anyone in the company can write a message of thanks to someone else and send it to that person. Would your people use a tool like that? The AT&T employees send over 30,000 of these each year.

Monsanto created an incredibly effective recognition program that also serves as a superior training tool. It published a book entitled *The Master Salesman* that contains the wit and wisdom of its top salespeople. Imagine the impact on the employees to be quoted in such a book. And also realize the helpful effect this advice provides to its new salespeople.

Combine recognition with training by compiling a booklet of your employees' on-the-job wisdom.

Many companies provide *Employee of the Month* awards to recognize those workers who go the extra mile. Let me suggest that you put a new twist on this. Rather than management selecting the recipient, have the peers vote on it. They know who is putting in the extra effort and making the greatest contribution.

Just the honor of being selected *Employee of the Month* is usually sufficient, but many companies will combine it with a plaque or small gift. There is a company in St. Louis that does a noteworthy thing for its *Employee of the Month*. The person is given a parking space near the front door, right by the president's reserved space[1].

Look for ways to increase the value of peer recognition; it doesn't have to cost you a penny.

Know the Names of Your People

Can you believe this is actually included? Sadly, there are some businesses where managers actually have a problem knowing the names of their employees. It is as if the nametags are as much for the management's benefit as for the customers. (As I think about this, I become convinced that the nametags really are for the management's benefit. When have you, as a customer, had the need to know the name of a restaurant worker?)

Best Tip
Do your best to know the name of all your people. A person's name is, to him or her, the sweetest word in the language.

I was in a fast-food restaurant last summer during a busy lunch rush. I was waiting for my order when I witnessed the manager try to get the attention of a kid working the drive-thru. "Hey, you," he kept shouting. Finally he asked a nearby worker, "What's *that* one's name?" (He didn't say "his." He actually referred to him as a "that.")

This silliness does not just occur in fast-food places. I am aware of one *Fortune* 500 company that sees turnover among its sales staff approaching 70 percent. Because of the probability that any individual salesperson will soon leave the company, staffers openly admit: "We don't really bother getting to know them all that well, because they're not going to be here long." Now which is the cause and which is the effect?

---

[1] Now in this context I should probably gush about how nice this is, but I frankly have a real problem with the president having a reserved space by the front door. If he wants such a convenient place to park, then he should either arrive at the office early every morning or get himself voted Employee of the Month. But, I digress.

We do have to be realistic. There are only so many names any human can legitimately remember. Maybe it is not possible for you to know all 1,500 people who work under your leadership. But it is the *desire* to know your employees that matters, because it flows over into other efforts you make in developing your company's culture. The desire to know them as individuals will lead you to make other decisions that do focus on caring about people individually.

Fred Smith, founder and CEO of FedEx, made a statement that gives great insight into both his character and the culture he cultivated at FedEx. He said, "The saddest day of my career was when I realized that the company had become so big it was no longer possible to know the names of all my employees." What kind of management team do you think he built with a philosophy like that?

Try to know everyone's name. This may not be realistic, but the simple *act* of trying will cause you to value your employees as individuals and treat them in a manner that encourages long tenure.

Title Creatively

Do not underestimate the importance of job titles and other symbols of prestige. The Chinese army once did away with all symbols of rank. Gone were the gleaming stars and distinctive emblems that declared that certain individuals had achieved success and power. But a new form of rank soon appeared. In place of the medals and stripes were various arrangements of chest-pocket pens. The color, size, and number of a person's pens indicated his rank.

One employer tried an exercise. He offered applicants the choice between the title of sales manager or salesperson. Although the salesperson job paid a bit more, most people took the sales manager position.

Some situations cannot permit the development of new titles. The military, for instance, would frown on creating any new ranks,

RETENTION IN ACTION: WALT DISNEY WORLD

No company believes more in recognizing their employees than Walt Disney World. They literally have 180 separate programs for employee recognition! One of these is called the *Spirit of Fred Award*, named for an employee named Fred. When Fred went from an hourly worker to a salaried position, five people taught him the values necessary for career success at Disney. This inspired the award, in which FRED became an acronym for *Friendly, Resourceful, Enthusiastic, and Dependable.*

This award was initially just a lark. But now it has developed significant prestige and is highly desired in the company. Even more prestigious is the *Lifetime Fred Award*—a bronze statue of Mickey Mouse given to multiple recipients of the *Spirit of Fred Award.*

and I doubt the other senators would appreciate one of their members calling herself *Supreme Commanding Senator.* But most situations do present some flexibility. Tenured sales people could have *Senior* added to their title. Expert technicians can become *Master Technicians*, and so forth. Consider your options with rewarding your people with more prominent titles. While they may not immediately show their excitement, you can be assured that they will wear such a designation with considerable pride.

Let Them Know Their Place

People need to know what their company is trying to do and why such an endeavor is worthwhile. You can't expect people to support a group if they don't agree with where it's headed or don't even know where it's headed. Carefully and fully explain to your team:

- Your vision for the future.

- Your strategy for getting there.
- Why this is the best strategy.
- Every achievement that indicates your team is reaching its goals.

But you must take this a step further. People can get lost in the bureaucracy of companies, especially those that are large with many layers of management. A person will feel insignificant if she does not know how she contributes to the overall corporate mission. Workers will be unfulfilled if they do not view their role as having an impact.

Explain to each employee how his or her job contributes to the organization. Show how the company's success is impacted by *each* person's contribution. Do not be afraid of being overly dramatic in your evaluation. The theme of "For want of a shoe, the horse was lost; for want of a horse, the battle was lost . . ." is dramatic, but accurate. You should have no trouble explaining each person's critical role in the organization, even if that organization has a million employees.

(Note that even though the United States military has a stockpile of nuclear weapons, countless jets, tanks and aircraft carriers, how does it promote itself in its recruiting advertisements? *An Army of one.*)

An excellent time to describe each person's important role is during individual performance reviews. Normally, these reviews are used to do a checklist of ratings for that person's performance during the previous year, with the sole objective being to decide how big of a raise to give them. Expand on this. Use this time to let her know how significant she is. And, use the review structure to demonstrate how she can make an even greater contribution.

While We Are on the Subject of Performance Reviews

Let's talk a bit more about performance reviews. As mentioned, these events are often underused. What stands as a magnificent opportunity to expand our people's talents is often relegated to a perfunctory exercise in filling out boilerplate forms.

Good managers take full advantage of this formal opportunity to communicate with their people. Yes, you should evaluate their performance. And, as we discussed in the last section, use the time to let them know their value to the company. But also use the event as a chance to make development plans for your employees. Review their interests and goals. Design a plan that includes college courses, company projects, and outside seminars that will help them reach those goals. Give them books to devour, such as titles from the *Agile Manager Series*, which will help them master new business skills.

Constantly look for opportunities to develop your people. The annual performance review is a great time to address the need each employee has for personal fulfillment.

Help Your Employees Self-Actualize

Earlier, we looked at the need for companies to provide benefits to the employee. Look at some of these. Retirement benefits, hospitalization insurance, company softball team, medical leave, sabbaticals, vacations . . . what do these have in common? You have to *leave* work in order to enjoy them!

Companies must look inward to satisfy their employees. A person spends more of his waking hours with his job than his family. If you want to keep him part of *your* family, you must provide work incentives that motivate, challenge, and interest him.

People must feel they are growing, learning, and progressing. Modern business structure, with fewer employees at small firms and flatter management structures at larger ones, makes it difficult to fulfill this need. But it's important that you do try to fill this need because your best employees are the ones who most feel the need to learn.

Your people should not feel that they must look elsewhere in order to develop their careers. An employee who has an attrac-

---

Retention in Action: General Electric

Every spring, the top officers at GE spend three weeks combing through the resumés of its current executives. These executives prepare internal resumés listing their accomplishments, strengths, and ideal next moves. The brass chooses 360 professionals to be taught by the company's highest executives about what it takes to succeed at GE.

There is another program for general management hopefuls. Teams of students tackle some of GE's most aggravating business problems and later make a presentation to the corporate executive council. Still another executive development course is held annually where aspiring company officers dissect critical issues facing the company.

GE believes that giving people the chance to develop within the company will keep them with the company for their entire careers. This is not always the case: GE is an attractive source for other companies to shop for chief executives. But General Electric's 8 percent turnover rate suggests that this focus on internal development is an unmitigated success in retaining its people.

---

tive vision of his future with your company is far less apt to leave. It is certainly true that each person should take responsibility for the development of his or her own career, but providing a clear career path is the responsibility of the company.

Let's look at an example of a company taking that responsibility seriously. The Revere Group, a technology consulting firm in Chicago, knows it's hard to grow a company if the employees don't grow, too. So it has a career-pathing program designed to both retain and grow talent. Employees meet annually with a company-assigned mentor to develop an individual development plan. That plan determines how the employee will spend her required two weeks of training as well as what progress she needs to make to receive a promotion or change jobs.

Employees receive regular updates on their progress and have an ongoing relationship with their mentors. Note that there is nothing complicated or magical about this program. It consists simply of open communication and an organized approach to developing the employee. The employee has no doubt that his company cares about his career development and is willing to be an active partner in achieving those goals.

> **Best Tip**
>
> Provide on-the-job incentives that challenge, motivate, and interest the employee. If you're successful, you'll keep the person for a long, long time.

Obtain the Highest Level of Employee Commitment

People develop an absolute, unbreakable loyalty when they feel that they are part of something greater than they are—that they are doing something important in the world. How else do you explain the low turnover rate among missionaries and Peace Corps volunteers? It sure ain't the money!

Some companies and organizations have an easier time developing this image than others do. For instance, pharmaceutical companies create a mission to eliminate disease and suffering. The Air Force retains its pilots—despite opportunities for them to quadruple their income by joining commercial airlines—by appealing to patriotism.

On the other hand, some companies and jobs do not easily fit into this category. For instance, my father spent a forty-year career with Kimberly-Clark as a quality-control inspector. Since Delsy was one of its products, he referred to his occupation as a "toilet paper tester." This is not a situation where a worker can be motivated by feeling that he is involved in great goals. Or is it?

I can remember an evening that our family was watching television and a Kleenex commercial came on. You may remember it. In order to show how strong Kleenex was, the famous musician Harry James was blowing on a trumpet that had a wet tissue secured across the bell. No matter how loud he played, Harry James could not rip that Kleenex. Kimberly-Clark made its point: Kleenex could stand up to a sneeze. My dad had a proud grin cross his face. "You know, I was the one who tested and approved that Kleenex," he stated.

So was this factory worker with a funny title unimportant and beyond inspiration? No. In fact, he served a critical function that created a lasting impression of quality for his company.

You can create a sense of mission in your employees. Good managers will find this purpose and communicate it inspirationally to their team. This leadership will have a definite long-term impact on the retention of your employees.

I recall a television commercial for a department store. The store manager was holding a brief meeting with his sales team. He called an associate, Evelyn, to the front of the room while he recounted a telephone call he had just received from a customer. It seems that the customer—a father who had no clue as to what clothes to buy for his daughter—had been served by this salesperson. She quickly understood the problem and selected a half-dozen outfits for the little girl. "And then," the manager related, "Evelyn helped the young lady put on a fashion show for her daddy that he will always remember. Way to go, Evelyn. That's what our service is all about."[2] That salesperson did reach a higher calling. And that sales manager was brilliant in how he used the story to inspire his team.

Redeploy Workers to Motivate

Redeployment was a novelty a decade ago. Today, close to 40 percent of American companies will redeploy their workers in new positions or departments rather than lose them to attractive offers.

---

[2] Yes, this is really corny. But as the father of a four-year-old daughter, I have to confess tearing up as I write this.

RETENTION IN ACTION: HOME DEPOT

Home Depot calls its employees *associates*. Lots of companies do that, and it is usually just a gimmick. But this company is built from the inside out—more than 90 percent of non-entry-level jobs are filled internally, and only twelve of the company's four hundred department heads were recruited from outside the company. As founders Bernie Marcus and Arthur Blank write in *Built from Scratch*, their history of the company, "*Associate* implies an equal as opposed to a wage slave. We value what the salesperson on the store floor says just as much—sometimes more—than what the district manager says. . . . The salesperson touches the customer more."

The company's stock purchase plan makes true associates of all employees. Everyone can buy stock at any time for a 15 percent discount off the company's stock price, which is set once a year.

While the company will not reveal its exact turnover statistics, a company spokesman says it is about 20 percent below that of the rest of the retail industry.

Many workers leave their jobs and are enticed elsewhere because they feel stagnant or just plain bored. Try to be proactive in keeping people aboard by encouraging them to progress in their careers under your same roof. A good way to do this is to post all internal job openings, clearly listing requirements and skills needed. Then go one step further and provide training in those skills. Employees will view your company as one that can supply their career needs and will not be as susceptible to wandering eyes.

AT&T addresses this issue with a program called *Resource Link*. In essence, this is an in-house temp service. Employees with a diversity of skills market their abilities for temporary assignment within other departments. This program helps fight boredom and job plateauing while making excellent use of the talents of existing employees. Not only does it reduce turnover, but the program also takes a knife to the cost of outside consultants. (Ouch.)

Enhance Jobs

Let's look at some other ways to enhance the nature of your employees' jobs.

Everyone gets a mentor. Start a mentoring program in which senior-level employees coach less-experienced employees. This, incidentally, will not only help develop the junior employee but will also expand the mentor's personal job growth.

Involve employees in planning their training. Again, here we get two for the price of one. Not only will employees benefit from the training, but they will also expand their skills by learning how to design training programs.

Enlist employees to provide in-house seminars. Everyone is an expert in something and you will be surprised at the depth of knowledge available in your own back yard. Discover your employees' expertise and encourage the development of in-house programs.

Find ways to make every job interesting. No one wants to do the same job over and over, day after day. And while all jobs will require some repetitive tasks, everyone should have at least a part of their job be of high interest to them.

Provide lots of information and insight. Information is power, and employees want to be empowered with the information they need to know to do their jobs better and more effectively. And, more than ever, employees want to know how they are doing in their jobs and how the company is doing in its business. Open the channels of communication in an organization to allow employees to be informed, ask questions, and share information.

Involve employees in all aspects of the company's goals. Managers today are faced with an incredible number of opportunities and problems. As the speed of business continues to increase dramatically, the amount of time that they have to make decisions continues to decrease. Involving employees in decision making, especially when the decisions affect them directly, is respectful, practical, and productive.

Give them some breathing room. Few people want to be closely monitored. Workers want the flexibility to do their jobs as they see fit. Giving people some space increases the chance that they will perform well, as well as bring additional initiative, ideas, and energy to their jobs.

Give employees their fifteen minutes. Everyone appreciates getting credit when it is due. Occasions to share the successes of employees with others are almost limitless. Newsletter articles, bulletin board postings, internal memos, press releases to the local paper . . . as I said, the options available are legion.

The Agile Manager's Checklist

✔ Never forget: Employees look to their jobs to supply a sense of fulfillment and value.

✔ There are many low- and no-cost ways to show your appreciation. Use those listed in this chapter, then think up some on your own.

✔ For maximum motivation, let people know where the company is headed and why. Show how they fit into the vision.

✔ Ensure people feel they are growing, learning, and progressing.

✔ To motivate and challenge on an ongoing basis, regularly make jobs bigger in terms of breadth and responsibility.

✔ The best motivator is also without cost. Look the employee in the eye and say, "Thank you."

Chapter Eight

*F*ight Back

"Never confuse motion with action."

—Dr. Martin Luther King, Jr.

"OK, calm down and catch your breath." The Agile Manager was on the phone with Katherine. She was reporting that three employees had told her they had been approached by a head-hunter about specific opportunities with MegaGlobal.

Katherine continued. "But there is some good news here. None of the people I talked with have any intention of jumping ship. I guess we're safe for now."

The Agile Manager paused for a few moments to consider the situation. "Katherine, let me explain what is happening," the Agile Manager began. "MegaGlobal is raiding us. They have seen that things have shaped up and realize that we employ a lot of great people. So they are going after our people, using a shotgun approach. For every person that you know about, I'll bet there have been a dozen we don't know about. Yet."

"In a way," Katherine commented, "this raid is a compliment to our company."

That's a real healthy way to look at things, the Agile Manager *thought, but I had rather that they had sent flowers. "Yes, it is a tribute to how well things have been going, but we've got to take some serious action. Let me discuss what you have told me with Jim, and then I'll call you right back and let you know when we'll be arriving at your office."*

"You make it sound like we're preparing for war," Katherine observed.

"That we are," replied the Agile Manager. "That we are."

We have explored employee motivation, quality corporate retention programs, and generational incentives. These will all help you develop your thoughts about retaining employees as well as setting up programs in your company that should make a strong impact.

But now let's take this final chapter and explore some special circumstances. Among other things, let's look at how to save poor performers. Let's look at how you might get a resigning employee to rethink his decision. And let's consider ways to deal with a situation where your company is being raided by a competitor. In other words, let's fight back.

'Good' Turnover

Many experts will advise you to separate turnover into two classes, *good* and *bad*. Bad turnover is when excellent employees quit. Good turnover is when bad employees are fired or when a worker retires.

I strongly disagree with this categorization. Turnover is turnover and the effect on your company is the same no matter whether the employee is a strong performer pirated by your competitor, a poor employee who has not lived up to his potential, or a solid worker who retires. You want to hold on to your people. Period.

But what about the poor worker? Shouldn't we move to quickly rid ourselves of these slugs? No. While this may be the eventual outcome, it should not be your initial focus. You should first seek to turn his performance around. You should fire him if you are unable to turn the performance around, but doing so should be viewed as a management failure rather than "good" turnover.

What about the retiring worker? How is this a *failure* of management? OK, this might not be a failure of management, but it is often a missed opportunity for success. We'll start this discussion by looking at ways to retain retiring workers.

Retaining the Retiring Worker

In the coming years, as Boomers continue to age and retire, pressures on America's job bank will only increase. To protect their employment base, companies must implement new ways to attract and to retain mature employees.

Let's realize who we are talking about here. Retirement-age workers are often your most valuable employees. Generally speaking, they are more punctual and reliable than younger workers. They take pride in their work and demonstrate a work ethic from a previous generation. They are more patient, which can be of enormous help in dealing with customers and training of new employees. And, they are already

Best Tip

Try to turn performance around before you get rid of a less-than-ideal worker. It's cheaper than hiring anew.

trained and well seasoned. This saves you enormous training costs as you benefit from your training investments rather than adding to them.

The fact is that most retiring workers want to continue working. A 1996 study conducted by the *American Association of Retired Persons* showed that 60 percent of those polled wanted to work post-retirement in one capacity or another.

Further, many retirement-aged adults *need* to work. They may have become divorced or widowed, and they vitally need supplemental income or insurance benefits. For others, the desire to work is not always driven by money. For instance, the married homemaker whose children have grown and left the house has a new set of values motivating her to work. Aside from supplemental income or benefits, the empty nester may be motivated by social relationships, a feeling of continued contribution, personal fulfillment and enrichment, as well as continually learning something new. They may simply want to keep busy.

Several leading companies have learned the advantage of retaining, *and even recruiting,* retirement-aged workers. For example General Electric has proven that it is more economical to retrain veteran engineers in new technologies than to hire new ones. Days Inn has found that recruiting older workers has had a positive effect on both sales and service. This is the same thing that Walt Disney World has seen and is the reason a substantial portion of its workforce is composed of retirees of other corporations. And Travelers Group has actually developed a job bank for both its retirees and those of other companies.

Retaining the Retiree

Consider these methods for holding on to the people who have decades of experience in solving your company's problems:

Convert jobs to part-time. PricewaterhouseCoopers conducted a survey. "If you were offered a plan to transition from full-time employment to part-time employment before retiring completely, would you like to take advantage of it?" 82 percent answered yes. Eighty-two percent! Realize what this means. You could hold on to the experience and deep knowledge of these workers while only paying them part-time wages. This represents an incredible return on your investment and a smart use of your resources.

Hire them as consultants. By allowing eligible employees to retire and be rehired as consultants, you can provide the worker with the best of both worlds. The rehired consultants could supplement their income by tapping into their pensions as well as performing duties that allow flexible work hours. You can also benefit from this flexibility by designing a job-scope that only encompasses the use of their *prime* knowledge (rather that paying for some of the more routine activities).

Save the Poor Performer

I had a humbling experience early in my career. I was telling my boss about one of my managers who had a poor attitude. I declared that he should be fired because, "You know, you just can't turn around a bad attitude."

He replied, "Ken, the reason why you can't turn around a bad attitude is because you have never tried." Ouch.

How many people have been fired who could have been saved by good managers? Perhaps the complete solution goes beyond the scope of this book[1], but let's discuss some ways to reduce turnover by saving poor performers.

> **Best Tip**
>
> You're losing a lot when you lose someone to retirement. Entice him to stay by converting the job to part time.

First, let me make this clear: I am not saying that in order to lower turnover you should lower your standards or ignore serious policy infractions. Quite the contrary, you can often improve overall retention by firing a few deadbeat workers or poor managers.

But I am not addressing the occasional situation in which a worker is unsavable. I am stating unequivocally that the overwhelming majority of poor performers can be saved if reasonable efforts are applied. Consider these options:

Have a direct conversation. This is such a basic element of good management that it may seem that there is no need to even mention it. But you would be shocked at how often employees are surprised to learn that they are performing poorly. Never

---

[1] Though I do recommend that you read other *Agile Manager* titles, such as *Coaching to Maximize Performance* and *Managing Irritating People*.

leave the employee in the dark. Ask the employee to evaluate his own performance. Don't be surprised if he gives himself a glowing review. Be kind, but direct. Let him know that things are not as they seem and that you are disappointed.

Best Tip

Train to improve poor skills. A lack of skills is one of the easiest performance problems to solve.

Say clearly that you believe in him and his abilities. Set up a plan of action that will bring him up to standards and provide him every tool he could possibly need to meet that standard. Odds are favorable that this employee will be saved if he understands what must be improved and you commit to help him making that improvement.

Change the scenery. Sometimes a good employee simply finds herself in the wrong spot. Things don't click. She may be in the wrong department or have the wrong boss. Perhaps the chemistry with co-workers is all wrong or they just got off on the wrong foot. Give her a change of scenery, a new boss or a new set of peers. Often this relocation will allow her to hit on all cylinders and she will demonstrate the potential you saw at the interview.

Require a mentor. Some people do not respond to their boss no matter how hard the manager tries or how advanced his skills. Yet these same workers may respond to a mentor or a peer. Assign the problem employee to a peer with excellent performance and quality work habits. The employee will often catch on to the program, mirror the mentor's work ethic and begin erasing the bad habits.

Address any lack of skills. Poor job skills are just about the easiest performance problem there is to deal with. Assuming the worker wants to do the job well, then all that is required is education. Provide informal peer demonstrations, on-site skill seminars or formal classroom instruction. Whatever is reasonably required should be provided. The cost of such training is minimal especially when you amortize it over the long tenure of a saved employee.

Put the deficient skill in its true perspective. How significant is it within the total scope of the particular job? Consider how strong the employee might be in other aspects of their job. For example, a factory department manager may be poor at writing weekly reports but first-rate at maintaining quality production runs. His overall strengths may far outweigh the administrative weaknesses. Sometimes it is acceptable for the employee to have a serious weakness, as long as you are aware of the problem and are able to redesign the workload.

When an Employee Resigns

We have spent most of this book talking about prevention. But what about an immediate problem? Someone just walked into your office, handed you an envelope and said, "I want to let you know that I am giving notice. I am resigning to go to work for MegaGlobal Competition, Inc." Now, what do you do?

Sadly, the chance of retaining this employee is remote. Once the employee has reached this commitment, it is difficult to uncover all her true reasons, counter the new suitor's advances and re-motivate her about working for your company. Saving her is a longshot, but let's look at how we might take our best retention effort. You have to have a plan and a system. Here's mine:

1. **Declare this as your top priority.** Commit to this being your only project for the next few days. Saving this employee is your complete focus. Cancel all other meetings; postpone any trips. Make sure the employee knows how important this situation is to

Best Tip

When faced with a resignation, uncover the real reasons for the departure and then address them systematically to save the employee.

you and the company. (This in itself may do the trick. Many

people are vulnerable to companies that approach them because they feel that no one really cares.)

2. Gather all information. Listen to the employee. Ask questions until you have a complete understanding of what lead to the decision, how she was approached, and all the terms of her new employment. You have to know the full truth, even if that truth hurts your personal feelings.

3. Contact your boss immediately. Explain the situation to him in detail and solicit his involvement in saving the employee. Once again, check your ego. Hide no facts, even if the reason she quit is because she can't stand you as a boss.

4. Use all your assets. Involve your boss, the HR department, the employee's mentor and anyone else that you feel may have influence.

5. Keep the resignation secret. Many people actually want to change their minds, but fear losing face if word has already leaked out to the masses. Do everything you can to keep this out of the headlines. Now, I know that it's a bit unrealistic to think that no one knows about the resignation, but there is a real difference between a whispering grapevine and general public knowledge.

> ## Best Tip
>
> Keep resignations as secret as you can. If word leaks out, the employee may depart just to save face.

6. Solve the employee's problems. Quitting is not a natural action for an employee; something must drive them to action. By now you should fully understand what led to this resignation and you must be prepared to fix the problems.

Please note: If, after evaluating the issues you feel that some problems are not legitimate, or you are not willing to make *all* the necessary changes, then stop your efforts right there. Do not try to retain the employee by solving some of his problems and ignoring others. This situation will not permit a partial fix. Either be willing to fix the situation completely or shake her hand

and wish her the best in her new job.

7. Slam the door on the competition. Once the employee agrees to stay with your company, you should make sure the competitor knows that the final bell has rung. Have the employee send a certified letter to the other company, declaring that she has changed her mind and that the decision (this time) is final. She should make it clear that they should not contact her further. You should, of course, help the employee compose this letter.

Now, sadly, I must return you to earth and remind you that there is still about a 75 percent chance that you will lose this employee within a year. An employee is never really the same once she has been led along the path of resignation. She will never view your company in the same light and your company's relationship with her will never be quite the same. You will also find that you never look at her in the same way. Subconsciously you may even resent how she "twisted your arm" and "slyly manipulated" you into all those concessions.

Sigh. It is not pleasant to contemplate, but you are human. That's just the way it usually ends up. Which is why you should put such great efforts into prevention as opposed to reaction.

When Your Organization Has Been Targeted

There are two reasons that a headhunter would target a company for raiding its employees. First, the company has serious problems and the employees are vulnerable. The second, the company has a stellar record in managing its people and the employees are quite desirable. Either situation may cause your company to become the victim of an organized raid.

How should you react? Depending on the root cause, you will either be insulted or flattered. Once you have dealt with the ego issues, you must take action. Here are some successful tactics:

- As a preventive measure, periodically hire some of the larger recruiting firms to complete assignments for you. Ethics will prevent them from approaching any of your employees within one year of working for you.

- Have your CEO call theirs and ask him to call off the dogs. You will be surprised how often companies will retreat when civilly asked to do so at the highest level.

- Train your receptionist on the importance of not supplying names to outsiders. Block easy access to organizational charts and telephone directories by declaring them the confidential documents that they are.

- Send an employee to interview with the competitor. Learn what their tactics are and what sales pitch is being used.

Threaten to Sue

Well, this is America, right? We are a litigious society and sometimes this nuclear tactic works like a sledgehammer killing cockroaches. The courtroom has become a great equalizer in business. Take the example of (relatively) tiny Informix Software. They sued giant Oracle for theft of trade secrets after Oracle hired a dozen of its engineers. Informix later dropped the suit, but the threat of the hassle of legal action caused Oracle to move on to other prey. Also, when word hit the streets that Informix was fighting back, other companies decided to avoid the hassle and instead hunt more passive game.

> **Best Tip**
>
> Understand that if a head-hunter targets your firm, you have structural weaknesses that make you vulnerable to employee pilfering. Strengthen yourself!

I must admit to having been personally tamed by these tactics. A new company was entering the Atlanta market. It retained my firm to conduct an extensive search for dozens of managers. I targeted several companies that were similar to my client and was having considerable success in attracting their managers. One afternoon I received a certified letter from one target's attorney. In essence, he "ordered" me to stop approaching its managers, claiming that I was interfering with an employment contract and that he would do all sorts of wicked things to me if I didn't back off.

Now, I knew that their managers were not under any contract. And I knew that Georgia's tortious interference laws did not even remotely apply to this situation. And I suspect that the lawyer knew that I knew his letter was nothing more than a waste of some good 100 percent cotton paper. While my first instinct was to fight, I instead decided to stop recruiting its people. Why go through the hassle when there were so many other companies that wouldn't lift a finger to defend their people?

Handle Mergers Intelligently

An interesting thing happens when people worry about losing their jobs. They quit. Chapter five discusses this phenomenon, but let's address a practical application of this problem affecting a successful, growing company. Let's discuss how to keep your workforce when you acquire or merge with another company.

Usually, a high-quality workforce is one of the attractions for a company to acquire another. But the time between the merger announcement and the actual acquisition date is one of great stress to the workers. Rumors run freely, usually declaring that everyone is going to get fired and "they" are going to bring all their

Best Tip

Address rumors about mergers immediately, especially if they are true. If you don't, many good people will feel they have no choice but to find another job.

people over to run things. Again, people get nervous and often hedge their bets by seeking other employment.

(In fact, headhunters smell blood in the water during this time. They know workers are vulnerable and will target the employees of any company being acquired.)

Acknowledge this situation whenever you are involved in a merger or acquisition. Make dealing with it an integral part of the merger process. Again, the employees are probably one of the main reasons for the acquisition. Do all you can to protect this asset. Here are some steps to consider:

- Openly discuss this issue with the existing management team of the acquired company. Let them know your intentions and that you value the people. Keep in mind that the selling company is usually trying to protect its existing employees, so it should be quite easy to make retention a team effort.
- The leadership group of the acquiring company should spend some time, either individually or in small groups, with *each* employee of the acquired company. Let them get to know your faces and hear you answer their questions directly.
- Explain your policies, compensation structure, and benefits. Also, clearly discuss your company's culture, values, and goals.
- Invite spouses to meetings so that they can also have their fears addressed.
- Honor all tenure that the employees have earned with the acquired company. If you make them start all over, they will feel, legitimately, that they have been conquered rather than merged. They really have no reason to stay if they lose their status and seniority.
- If there are to be layoffs or terminations, work quickly and use a sharp knife. Get it over with in one day, announce what happened and make it clear that the carnage is over.
- And on the acquisition date, celebrate! Make this an exciting event dedicated to declaring these employees full members of your team.
- Above all else, communicate, communicate, communicate.

The Agile Manager's Checklist

✔ There's no such thing as "good" turnover. All employees are worth saving.

✔ To save poor performers, try assigning them a mentor. A mentor can often make gains that a boss can't.

✔ Don't accept resignations without doing something to save the relationship. Start by listening.

✔ Once you have saved an employee who was about to resign, have her send a certified letter to the hiring company clearly stating her intention to remain with your company.

✔ When you start losing employees to a headhunter or competitor, fight back. Start by addressing the reasons people are leaving.

Coda

"*Employers have to understand that if they want to attract and keep good people, they've got to treat those people as whole people who have lives outside work. They've got to respect those lives in their entirety. They can't treat employees as costs of doing business. They have to understand that they're critical, valuable assets and those assets have to be nurtured in every way.*"

—ROBERT REICH

Whatever happened to the simple equation of an honest day's work for an honest day's pay? Well, it disappeared about the time of the McKinley assassination. Work is no longer just something done to put bread on the table. We look to our jobs not just for cash, but for entertainment, identity, fulfillment, and cultural belonging. You can argue the anthropology all you want, but for the last hundred years work has rivaled family and religion as a core human need. The worker needs the employer.

You would expect that, given these circumstances, workers

would be clinging to their jobs. Yet, attrition has grown to alarming rates. Why the disconnect? Don't blame the worker; we have been running them off.

For too long the subject of retention has been on the corporate credenza. Business plans treat retention as an ancillary social objective rather than as a core business requirement. Usually, this issue has been delegated to the human resources department as a side project meant to show a company's creativity and compassion. But retention is not a human resource issue; it is a management issue.

We have seen the incredible expense that high turnover burdens a business with. We know the impact on people's lives. We understand the direct correlation between high retention and high profits.

High attrition is a disease as preventable as lung cancer and every bit as devastating. And just like the disease, we bring it on ourselves and overlook the consequences until it has a fatal lock on the corporate body.

American business must approach the subject of attrition with the same alarm it would deal with any other business crisis. Just like high bank interest rates. Just like an oil shortage. Only this problem is different. It is infinitely solvable.

I have presented numerous tangible actions you can take to solve your company's attrition issues. I focused on this because I believe that specific action steps are the reason you bought this book. But to get to the root of the problem, to truly hurdle the obstacle, you must also contemplate some of the theory included in the text. Pay special attention to these intangibles because they are the ultimate solutions to this problem.

- Realize that high retention equals high profits. Every time.
- You do not have to have a turnover crisis to reap the benefits of lowered turnover.
- Treat all employees with respect.
- Understand that people are different and so are their needs.

- Provide for those specific and individual needs.
- Value the older worker and bridge their retirement.
- Never write anyone off. Nearly anyone can be saved.
- Develop your people. This is as much a personal need for them as it is a manpower solution for you.
- If people like their bosses, they stay. If they don't, they leave.

The fact is, people *want* to stay with your company. All we have to do is stop running them off. You've got the tools to do that. Start saving employees—now—and reap the benefits.